sockupied

20 **KNIT PROJECTS**
to Satisfy your **Sock Obsession**

Edited by **Anne Merrow**

INTERWEAVE
interweave.com

EDITORS: Anne Merrow with Ann Budd

DESIGN: Karla Baker

PHOTOGRAPHY: Harper Point Photography,
Joe Coca, Joe Hancock, Ann Sabin Swanson

PRODUCTION: Katherine Jackson

Interweave
A division of F+W Media, Inc.
4868 Innovation Drive
Fort Collins, CO 80525
interweave.com

Manufactured in China by RR Donnelley Shenzhen.

Library of Congress Cataloging-in-Publication Data
Sockupied : 20 knit projects to satisfy your sock obsession / editor,
Anne Merrow with Ann Budd.
pages cm
ISBN 978-1-62033-795-0 (pbk.)
ISBN 978-1-62033-796-7 (PDF)
1. Knitting--Patterns. 2. Socks. I. Budd, Ann, 1956-, editor of
compilation. II. Merrow, Anne, 1977-, editor of compilation. III. Title:
20 knit projects to satisfy your sock obsession. IV. Title: Sockupied.
TT825.S665 2014
746.43'2--dc 3
2014005780

*5578 9761
9/14*

10 9 8 7 6 5 4 3 2 1

ACKNOWLEDGMENTS

Sockupied has been fortunate to rely on the talents of a variety of designers, editors, and photographers. Thanks to Tricia Waddell, Marilyn Murphy, Amy Palmer, Eunny Jang, Anita Osterhaug, TJ Harty, Ian Frizzell, and the Tenfold Collective for getting the first issue off the ground. The talented Pamela Norman designed the initial look and feel, and Susan Hazel Rich, Kit Kinseth, and Charlene Tiedemann have helped it evolve. Photographers Joe Hancock, Joe Coca, and Harper Point's Nate Rega captured every sock to its best advantage. Our deepest gratitude is reserved for the writers and designers whose articles, patterns, and creative ideas have made every issue fun.

CONTENTS

Introduction 7

Ann's Go-To Socks 9

Azurea Socks 13

Caret + Chevron Socks 19

Speed Bump Socks 25

Flutterby Socks 29

✳ *Get Your Cast-On!* 36

Oak + Acorn Socks 43

Twisted Diamonds Socks 47

✳ *Cast-Ons For Comfy Cuffs* 50

Emerging Cable Socks 55

Spectrum Socks 63

✳ *Stranded Color Knitting in Socks* 66

Cataphyll Socks 71

Wyeast Socks 81

✳ *Sock Conversions* 84

Uloborus Socks 91

Simply Elegant Cable Socks 97

Turnalar Socks 101

Muscadine Socks 109

✳ *Bind-Offs for Toe-Up Socks* 112

Frost Feather Stockings 117

Schwäbische Socks 123

✳ *Top (Down) Toes* 128

Our Paths Cross Socks 133

Passerine Socks 143

Escadaria Socks 147

✳ *Save Your Socks* 154

Glossary 158

Designers 165

Yarn Sources 166

Index 167

INTRODUCTION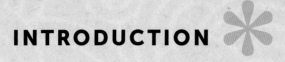

Sock knitting is **personal**.

When you're knitting socks, chances are you're making them for your own treasured toes or those of someone you know well (and like a lot). Even if you're not going to wear the finished socks, the process of knitting itself involves your hands, your brain, and your heart. With so much committed to that one pair of socks, you should be able to make them just the way you like them. Whether it's improving the fit or making them more fun to knit, *Sockupied* has always been about taking control of your sock knitting.

Sockupied was first published in 2010 as an all-digital, fully interactive publication called an eMag. Incorporating pop-ups, slide shows, videos, bells, and whistles, it has explored the possibilities of presenting socks in new media. With so many print publications going digital, it might seem strange to take an eMag into print. But when you're "in pursuit of sock knitting 24/7," as we are, there are times when even the ever-present computer or tablet isn't in your knitting bag charged up and ready to go. Socks are ancient technology; there's a place for knitting socks unplugged, too.

Since its first issue, *Sockupied* has celebrated the creative, colorful community of sock knitters and designers. In this collection we chose 20 patterns that represent the diversity of the first 10 issues: easy and difficult, handpainted and solid, cables and lace, toe-up and top-down . . . To accompany the patterns, we have also included some of our articles on sock-knitting fundamentals, including techniques that are designed to help you tweak patterns to suit your feet and your knitting style. Try out a different toe than the one you know best. Opt for a cuff other than the one in the pattern. Take matters into your own hands by converting a toe-up pattern to a top-down one (or vice versa).

Whether you prefer your patterns on screen or on paper, you can knit socks any way you like. And if you strike out on your own path, ignoring the pattern altogether and making socks that suit you, we won't mind at all.

Ann's Go-To SOCKS

by Ann Budd

Although she designs deliciously complex socks, this simple ribbed sock pattern is the one Ann Budd turns to for most of the socks she knits for herself. The k3, p1 rib hugs the leg and instep and lets the colors of hand-dyed yarn show to best advantage.

FINISHED SIZE About 6½ (7½, 8, 8½, 9½)" (16.5 [19, 20.5, 21.5, 24] cm) foot circumference, with ribbing slightly stretched, and 7½ (8¼, 9½, 10¼, 11)" (19 [21, 24, 26, 28] cm) foot length from back of heel to tip of toe. Socks shown measure 8" (20.5 cm) foot circumference.

YARN Fingering weight (Super Fine #1). *Shown here:* The Verdant Gryphon Bugga! (70% superwash merino, 20% cashmere, 10% nylon; 412 yd [377 m]/4 oz [113 g]): autumn tiger beetle, 1 (1, 1, 2, 2) skein(s).

NEEDLES *Upper leg:* U.S. size 1½ (2.5 mm): set of four double-pointed (dpn). *Lower leg and foot:* U.S. size 1 (2.25 mm): set of four dpn. *Adjust needle size if necessary to obtain the correct gauge.*

NOTIONS Markers (m); stitch holder (optional); tapestry needle.

GAUGE 32 sts and 44 rnds = 4" (10 cm) in St st on smaller needles.

notes

- These socks are worked from the top down; the rib pattern on the leg extends across the top of the instep.
- The upper half of the leg is worked on needles one half size larger than the size needed to obtain gauge.
- The end-of-round marker is placed before the last stitch on Needle 3 so that it doesn't fall off the end of the needle.
- Fine-tune the fit by adjusting the number of rounds worked in the foot before beginning the toe shaping.

Leg

With larger needles and using the Old Norwegian method (see page 50), CO 56 (64, 68, 72, 80) sts. Divide sts onto 3 dpn so that there are 12 (16, 16, 20, 24) sts on Needle 1, 32 (32, 36, 32, 32) sts on Needle 2, and 12 (16, 16, 20, 24) sts on Needle 3. Place a marker (pm) before last st on Needle 3 (see Notes), and join for working in the rnd. Rnds beg with first st on Needle 1 at back of leg.

SET-UP RND: *K3, p1; rep from *.

Work in k3, p1 rib as established until piece measures 3 (3¼, 3½, 3¾, 4)" (7.5 [8.5, 9, 9.5, 10] cm) from CO.

Change to smaller needles and cont in rib as established until piece measures 6 (6½, 6¾, 7½, 8¼)" (15 [16.5, 17, 19, 21] cm) from CO, or desired length to top of heel.

Heel

The heel is worked back and forth in rows on 28 (32, 34, 36, 40) sts centered over back of leg.

SET-UP ROW 1: (RS) Work 14 (16, 17, 18, 20) sts in established rib patt as foll: [K3, p1] 3 (4, 4, 4, 5) times, k2 (0, 1, 2, 0), turn work.

SET-UP ROW 2: (WS) Sl 1, p27 (31, 33, 35, 39)—28 (32, 34, 36, 40) heel sts.

Place rem 28 (32, 34, 36, 40) sts on holder to work later for instep or simply leave them unworked on one dpn.

HEEL FLAP

Work 28 (32, 34, 36, 40) heel sts back and forth in rows as foll:

ROW 1: (RS) *Sl 1 purlwise (pwise) with yarn in back (wyb), k1; rep from *.

ROW 2: (WS) Sl 1 pwise with yarn in front (wyf), purl to end.

Rep these 2 rows 13 (15, 16, 17, 19) more times—28 (32, 34, 36, 40) rows total; 14 (16, 17, 18, 20) chain-edge sts along each selvedge.

TURN HEEL

Work short-rows to shape heel cup as foll:

ROW 1: (RS) Sl 1, k15 (17, 18, 19, 21), ssk, k1, turn work.

ROW 2: (WS) Sl 1 pwise wyf, p5, p2tog, p1, turn.

ROW 3: Sl 1 pwise wyb, k6, ssk (1 st each side of gap formed on previous row), k1, turn.

ROW 4: Sl 1 pwise wyf, p7, p2tog (1 st each side of gap), p1, turn.

ROW 5: Sl 1 pwise wyb, k8, ssk, k1, turn.

ROW 6: Sl 1 pwise wyf, p9, p2tog, p1, turn.

ROW 7: Sl 1 pwise wyb, k10, ssk, k1, turn.

ROW 8: Sl 1 pwise wyf, p11, p2tog, p1, turn.

ROW 9: Sl 1 pwise wyb, k12, ssk, k1, turn.

ROW 10: Sl 1 pwise wyf, p13, p2tog, p1, turn.

Cont in this manner, working 1 more st before decreasing on each row and omitting last k1 on final RS row and last p1 on final WS row if there are not enough sts to work them (i.e., if you began with 28, 32, 36, or 40 sts)—16 (18, 20, 20, 22) heel sts rem.

SHAPE GUSSETS

Rejoin for working in the rnd as foll:

RND 1: With an empty needle (Needle 1) and RS facing, k16 (18, 20, 20, 22) heel sts, then pick up and knit (see Glossary) 14 (16, 17, 18, 20) sts through their back loops along edge of heel flap (1 st in each chain-edge st); with Needle 2, work 28 (32, 34, 36, 40) held instep sts in rib patt as established; with Needle 3, pick up and knit 14 (16, 17, 18, 20) sts through their back loops along other edge of heel flap (1 st in each chain-edge st), then knit the first 8 (9, 10, 10, 11) sts from Needle 1—72 (82, 88, 92, 102) sts total; 22 (25, 27, 28, 31) sts on Needle 1, 28 (32, 34, 36, 40) instep sts on Needle 2, 22 (25, 27, 28, 31) sts on Needle 3. Rnds beg with first st on Needle 1 at center of sole.

RND 2: On Needle 1, knit to last 3 sts, k2tog, k1 (p1, k1, k1, p1); on Needle 2, work 28 (32, 34, 36, 40) instep sts in rib patt as established; on Needle 3, k1 (p1, k1, k1, p1), ssk, knit to end—2 sts dec'd.

RND 3: On Needle 1, knit to last st, k1 (p1, k1, k1, p1); on Needle 2, work instep sts in rib patt as established; on Needle 3, k1 (p1, k1, k1, p1), knit to end.

Rep Rnds 2 and 3 (i.e., alternate a dec rnd with a plain rnd) 7 (8, 9, 9, 10) more times—56 (64, 68, 72, 80) sts rem.

Foot

Cont in patt as established until piece measures about 6 (6½, 7½, 8¼, 8¾)" (15 [16.5, 19, 20.5, 22] cm) from back of heel, or about 1½ (1¾, 2, 2, 2¼)" (3.8 [4.5, 5, 5, 5.5] cm) less than desired total foot length.

Toe

Change to St st on all sts and dec as foll:

RND 1: On Needle 1, knit to last 3 sts, k2tog, k1; on Needle 2, k1, ssk, knit to last 3 sts, k2tog, k1; on Needle 3, k1, ssk, knit to end—4 sts dec'd.

RND 2: Knit.

Rep Rnds 1 and 2 five (seven, eight, eight, nine) more times—32 (32, 32, 36, 40) sts rem.

Rep Rnd 1 every rnd (i.e., dec every rnd) 5 (4, 4, 5, 6) times—12 (16, 16, 16, 16) sts rem; 3 (4, 4, 4, 4) sts on Needle 1, 6 (8, 8, 8, 8) sts on Needle 2, 3 (4, 4, 4, 4) sts on Needle 3.

With Needle 3, knit the sts on Needle 1—6 (8, 8, 8, 8) sts each on 2 needles. Cut yarn, leaving a 10" (25.5 cm) tail.

Finishing

With tail threaded on a tapestry needle, use Kitchener st (see Glossary) to graft rem sts tog. Weave in loose ends and tighten up holes at gussets if necessary. Block lightly.

Azurea SOCKS

by Lorilee Beltman

Knitters whose calves or ankles don't fit into a standard sock size may have previously forgone the joys of sock knitting. With calves and ankles that can stretch to almost 150% of their resting circumferences, these socks give knitters with curvier legs a pattern that fits and looks great. A stacked flower pattern flows elegantly into the stretchy ribbed cuff.

FINISHED SIZE About 8 (8½, 9)" (20.5 [21.5, 23] cm) foot circumference, 9½ (10, 10½)" (24 [25.5, 26.5] cm) calf circumference, 9" (23 cm) height from bottom of heel to top of cuff, and 9" (23 cm) foot length from tip of toe. Foot length is adjustable. Socks shown measure 8½" (21.5 cm) foot circumference.

YARN Fingering weight (Super Fine #1). *Shown here:* (100% superwash merino wool; 450 yd [411 m]/4 oz [113 g]): #08 bermuda teal, 1 skein.

NEEDLES U.S. size 1 (2.5 mm): set of five double-pointed (dpn), two circular (cir), or one long cir. *Adjust needle size if necessary to obtain the correct gauge.*

NOTIONS Markers (m); tapestry needle.

GAUGE 30 sts and 48 rows = 4" (10 cm) in St st; 32 sts and 44 rnds = 4" (10 cm) in Stacked Tulip patt.

notes

* Sock is worked toe up and stretches to comfortably fit calf circumferences of 8½ to 13 (9 to 13½, 9½ to 14)" (21.5 to 33 [23 to 34.5, 24 to 35.5]) cm.

* Slip stitches purlwise with yarn held at wrong side of work, except where indicated otherwise.

* To accommodate different methods of working—double-pointed needles, two circulars, or one long circular—the stitches are divided into two halves, which are referred to as "instep" and "heel" stitches. "Instep" stitches cover the top of the foot and the front of the leg; these stitches are on the first of two double-pointed needles, first of two circular needles, or first half of one long circular needle. "Heel" stitches cover the bottom of the foot, the heel, and the back of the leg; these stitches are on the last two double-pointed needles, the second of two circular needles, or second half of one long circular needle.

Toe

With 12" (30.5 cm) tail over forefinger and bottom needle receiving the first st, CO 8 sts using Judy's Magic method (see Glossary).

RND 1: Holding tail tog with working yarn, knit—16 sts. Drop tail.

RND 2: Knit.

RND 3: [K1, (k1f&b; see Glossary) 2 times, k1] 4 times—24 sts.

RNDS 4 AND 5: Knit.

RND 6: [K2, (k1f&b) 2 times, k2] 4 times—32 sts.

RNDS 7–9: Knit.

RND 10: [K3, (k1f&b) 2 times, k3] 4 times—40 sts.

RNDS 11–13: Knit.

RND 14: [K4, (k1f&b) 2 times, k4] 4 times—48 sts.

RNDS 15–18: Knit.

RND 19: [K5, (k1f&b) 2 times, k5] 4 times—56 sts.

RNDS 20–23: Knit. Cont for your size as foll:

Size 8" (20.5 cm) only

RND 24: K28, [k6, (k1f&b) 2 times, k6] 2 times—60 sts: 28 sole sts and 32 instep sts.

RND 25: Knit. Skip to Foot.

Size 8½" (21.5 cm) only

RND 24: [K6, (k1f&b) 2 times, k6] 4 times—64 sts: 32 sole sts and 32 instep sts.

RND 25: Knit. Skip to Foot.

Size 9" (23 cm) only

RND 24: [K6, (k1f&b) 2 times, k6] 4 times—64 sts.

RNDS 25–27: Knit.

RND 28: [K7, (k1f&b) 2 times, k7] 2 times, k32—68 sts: 36 sole sts and 32 instep sts.

RND 29: Knit.

Foot

NEXT RND: K28 (32, 36) sole sts, work Row 1 of Stacked Tulip chart over 32 instep sts.

Cont in patt as established until foot measures 5" (12.5 cm) from tip of toe, or 4" (10 cm) less than total finished length, ending with an even-numbered chart row (make a note of last row worked).

Heel

SOLE FLAP

Sole flap is worked back and forth in rows over first 28 (32, 36) sts of rnd; last 32 sts will be worked later for instep.

NEXT ROW: (RS) K28 (32, 36), turn work.

NEXT ROW: (WS) P28 (32, 36), turn.

ROW 1: *Sl 1 (see Notes), k1; rep from * to end.

ROW 2: Sl 1, purl to end.

Rep Rows 1 and 2 twenty-two more times, then work Row 1 once more—48 rows total; 24 chain-edge sts along each selvedge.

Back of Leg

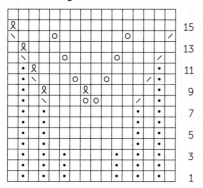

16 sts

Cuff

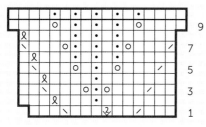

16 to 17 st repeat

Stacked Tulip

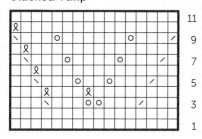

16 st repeat

☐	k
·	p
ℛ	k1tbl
O	yo
⤓	k1f&b
＼	ssk
／	k2tog
☐	pattern repeat

TURN HEEL

Work short-rows as foll:

SHORT-ROW 1: (WS) P16 (18, 20), ssp (see Glossary), p1, turn.

SHORT-ROW 2: (RS) [Sl 1, k1] 3 times, sl 1, k2tog, k1, turn.

SHORT-ROW 3: Sl 1, p7, ssp, p1, turn.

SHORT-ROW 4: Sl 1, k2, [sl 1, k1] 3 times, k2tog, k1, turn.

SHORT-ROW 5: Sl 1, p9, ssp, p1, turn.

SHORT-ROW 6: [Sl 1, k1] 5 times, sl 1, k2tog, k1, turn.

SHORT-ROW 7: Sl 1, p11, ssp, p1, turn.

SHORT-ROW 8: Sl 1, k2, [sl 1, k1] 5 times, k2tog, k1, turn.
Cont for your size as foll:

Size 8" (20.5 cm) only

SHORT-ROW 9: Sl 1, p13, ssp, p2—19 sts rem, turn.

SHORT-ROW 10: K1, [sl 1, k1] 9 times, do not turn. Skip to Shape Gussets.

Size 8½" (21.5 cm) only

SHORT-ROW 9: Sl 1, p13, ssp, p1, turn.

SHORT-ROW 10: [Sl 1, k1] 7 times, sl 1, k2tog, k1, turn.

SHORT-ROW 11: Sl 1, p15, ssp, p1, turn.

SHORT-ROW 12: Sl 1, k2, [sl 1, k1] 7 times, k2tog, k1, turn.

SHORT-ROW 13: P18, ssp, turn—19 sts rem.

SHORT-ROW 14: K1, [sl 1, k1] 9 times, do not turn. Skip to Shape Gussets.

Size 9" (23 cm) only

SHORT-ROW 9: Sl 1, p13, ssp, p1, turn.

SHORT-ROW 10: [Sl 1, k1] 7 times, sl 1, k2tog, k1, turn.

SHORT-ROW 11: Sl 1, p15, ssp, p1, turn.

SHORT-ROW 12: Sl 1, k2, [sl 1, k1] 7 times, k2tog, k1, turn.

SHORT-ROW 13: Sl 1, p17, ssp, p1, turn.

SHORT-ROW 14: [Sl 1, k1] 9 times, sl 1, k2tog, k1, turn.

SHORT-ROW 15: Sl 1, p19, ssp, turn.

SHORT-ROW 16: Ssk, [sl 1, k1] 8 times, sl 1, k2tog—19 sts rem, do not turn.

SHAPE GUSSETS

SET-UP RND: With RS facing, pick up and knit 26 sts along side of sole flap, place marker (pm), work 32 instep sts in patt as established, pm for beg of rnd, pick up and knit 26 sts along side of sole flap, knit to 1 st before m, p1, sl m, work in patt across instep sts—103 sts: 71 back-of-leg sts and 32 instep sts.

NEXT RND: P1, *k1, p1; rep from * to m, sl m, work 32 instep sts in patt as established.

DEC RND: P1, ssk, work in patt to 3 sts before m, k2tog, p1, sl m, work instep sts in patt—2 back-of-leg sts dec'd.

NEXT 2 RNDS: P1, k1, work in patt as established to 2 sts before m, k1, p1, sl m, work 32 instep sts in patt.

Rep last 3 rnds 6 (4, 2) more times, then work Dec rnd once more—87 (91, 95) sts rem: 55 (59, 63) back-of-leg sts and 32 instep sts.

Leg

Work even in patt until completing Row 5 of chart. Pm on each side of center 17 back-of-leg sts.

DEC RND: Work in patt to m, sl m, [k1, p1] 3 times, k1, k2tog, k2, [p1, k1] 3 times, sl m, work to m, sl m, work Row 6 of Stacked Tulip chart over 32 instep sts—86 (90, 94) sts rem: 54 (58, 62) back-of-leg sts and 32 front-of-leg (formerly instep) sts.

SET-UP RND: Work in patt to m, sl m, work Row 1 of Back of Leg chart over 16 sts, sl m, work to m, sl m, work Row 7 of Stacked Tulip chart over 32 front-of-leg sts.

Cont in patt as established through Row 16 of Back of Leg chart (and Row 11 of Stacked Tulip chart), then work Rows 1–11 of Stacked Tulip chart over all 86 (90, 94) sts 2 times, then work Rows 1 and 2 once more—piece measures about 6" (15 cm) from start of heel flap.

Cuff

DEC RND: Work in patt to m, sl m, work Row 1 of Cuff chart over 16 center back-of-leg sts, sl m, work to m, sl m, work Row 1 of Cuff chart over 32 front-of-leg sts—83 (87, 91) sts rem: 53 (57, 61) back-of-leg sts and 30 front-of-leg sts.

Cont in patt as established through Row 10 of chart—89 (93, 97) sts: 55 (59, 63) back-of-leg sts and 34 front-of-leg sts.

Rep Row 10 of chart 14 more times, or to desired length—piece measures about 9" (23 cm) from bottom of heel. Remove m. BO sts in patt using Jeny's Surprisingly Stretchy method (see Glossary).

Finishing

Weave in loose ends. Block lightly.

azurea socks

Caret + Chevron
SOCKS

by **Chrissy Gardiner**

These are socks designed to go both ways. Knitting top-down will result in chevrons that point down toward the toe, while knitting toe-up will result in chevrons that point toward the cuff. This is also a stitch pattern that's easily reversible, so you can simply flip the charts over and work them upside-down. See Sock Conversions, page 84, for more on reversing sock direction.

FINISHED SIZE About 8 (10)" (20.5 [25.5] cm) foot circumference (unstretched), 9¼ (10¼)" (23 [26] cm) from back of heel to tip of toe, and 6" (15 cm) from top of cuff to start of short-row heel. Leg and foot lengths are adjustable. To fit U.S. women's shoe sizes 6 to 8 (8 to 10). Socks shown measure 8" (20.5 cm) foot circumference; one is worked top-down and the other toe-up.

YARN Fingering weight (Super fine #1). *Shown here:* Schaefer Yarn Nichole (80% extrafine superwash merino, 20% nylon; 405 yd [370 m]/5 oz [142 g]): apple green, 1 skein for both sizes. *Note: This yarn has been discontinued.*

NEEDLES U.S. size 1.5 (2.5 mm): set of five double-pointed (dpn), two circular (cir), or one long cir. *Adjust needle size if necessary to obtain the correct gauge.*

NOTIONS Marker (m); tapestry needle.

GAUGE 16 sts and 24 rnds = 2" (5 cm) in St st.

notes

�֍ To accommodate different methods of working—double-pointed needles, two circulars, or one long circular—the stitches are divided into two halves, which are referred to as "instep" and "heel" stitches. "Instep" stitches cover the top of the foot and the front of the leg; these stitches are on the first of two double-pointed needles, first of two circular needles, or first half of one long circular needle. "Heel" stitches cover the bottom of the foot, the heel, and the back of the leg; these stitches are on the last two double-pointed needles, the second of two circular needles, or second half of one long circular needle.

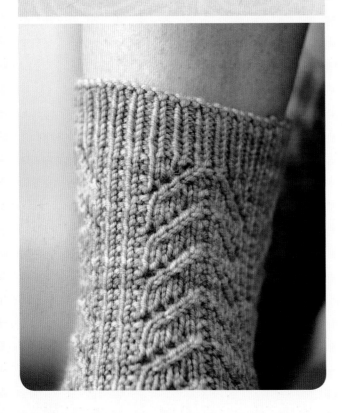

Top-Down Version

CUFF

CO 64 (80) sts. Divide sts (see Notes) as 33 (41) instep sts and 31 (39) heel sts.

Place marker (pm) and join for working in the rnd, being careful not to twist sts.

RIB RND: *P1, k1; rep from * to end.

Rep last rnd until piece measures 1" (2.5 cm) from CO.

LEG

Work the Leg chart for your size, working the 16 (20)-st patt rep 4 times for each rnd, until piece measures about 6" (15 cm) from CO for both sizes, or desired length to top of heel, ending with Rnd 6 of chart.

HEEL

Work Rnd 7 of Leg chart for your size over 33 (41) instep sts, but do not work heel sts.

note: If using dpns, place all heel sts on a single needle.

The heel is worked using short-rows (see Glossary) on the rem 31 (39) heel sts at end of rnd.

First Half

ROW 1: (RS) K30 (38), wrap next st, turn work.

ROW 2: (WS) P29 (37), wrap next st, turn.

ROW 3: Knit to 1 st before previously wrapped st (do not work any wrapped sts), wrap next st, turn.

ROW 4: Purl to 1 st before previously wrapped st (do not work any wrapped sts), wrap next st, turn.

Rep Rows 3 and 4 eight (eleven) more times—11 (13) unwrapped center sts; 10 (13) wrapped sts on each side of center sts.

Second Half

ROW 1: (RS) Knit to first wrapped st, knit wrap tog with wrapped st, turn.

ROW 2: (WS) Sl 1 purlwise with yarn in front (pwise wyf), purl to first wrapped st, purl wrap tog with wrapped st, turn.

ROW 3: Sl 1 pwise with yarn in back (wyb), knit to next wrapped st, knit wrap tog with wrapped st, turn.

ROW 4: Sl 1 pwise wyf, purl to next wrapped st, purl wrap tog with wrapped st, turn.

Instep, 10" (25.5 cm) Foot Circumference

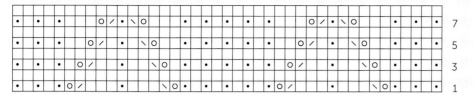

Instep, 8" (20.5 cm) Foot Circumference

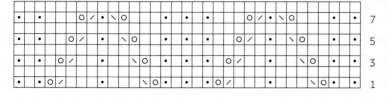

Legend:
- ☐ k
- • p
- ○ yo
- ╱ k2tog
- ╲ ssk
- ☐ pattern repeat

Leg, 10" (25.5 cm) Foot Circumference

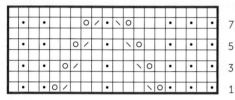

Leg, 8" (20.5 cm) Foot Circumference

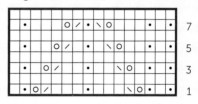

Rep Rows 3 and 4 seven (ten) more times—1 wrapped st rem at each end of heel needle.

NEXT ROW: (RS) Sl 1 pwise wyb, knit to last wrapped st, knit wrap tog with wrapped st, do not turn.

note: If using dpns, divide the heel sts on 2 dpns again.

NEXT RND: With RS still facing, work Rnd 8 of Leg chart for your size over 33 (41) instep sts, knit wrap at start of heel sts tog with wrapped st, knit to end of heel sts—64 (80) sts total; rnd now begins at side of foot at start of instep sts.

FOOT

NEXT RND: Work Rnd 1 of Instep chart for your size over across 33 (41) instep sts, knit to end of rnd.

Working 33 (41) instep sts in chart patt as established and heel sts in St st, work even until foot measures 2 (2½)" (5 [6.5] cm) less than desired finished length from back of heel to tip of toe, ending with Rnd 8 of Instep chart.

note: If ending on Rnd 8 causes the foot to be more than 2 (2½)" shorter than desired length, work in St st until foot measures 2 (2½)" less than desired length.

TOE

note: The short-row toe is worked on the heel/sole stitches the same as for the short-row heel. The first half of the short-rows are worked along the underside of the foot to the tips of the toes, then the second half of the short-rows are worked along the top of the foot from toe-tip to the base of the toes.

NEXT RND: Work instep sts as k1, ssk, k27 (35), k2tog, k1; do not work sts from heel/sole of foot yet—62 (78) sts total: 31 (39) sts each for instep and heel/sole.

Place 31 (39) heel/sole sts on one needle, if they are not already on a single needle, and work the first half and second half short-rows as for the heel until 1 wrapped st rem at each end of toe sts.

NEXT RND: With RS facing, sl 1 pwise wyb, knit to wrapped st, knit wrap tog with wrapped st, knit across 31 (39) instep sts, knit wrap at start of toe sts tog with wrapped st, knit to end of toe sts.

FINISHING

If necessary, arrange sts on two needles for instep and toe with 31 (39) sts on each needle. Use Kitchener st (see Glossary) to graft live sts tog on top of foot, across base of wearer's toes.

Weave in loose ends. Block lightly.

Toe-Up Version

TOE

note: The short-row toe is worked the same as for the top down version's short-row heel. The first half of the short-rows are worked along the top of the foot from the base of the toes to the toe-tips, and then the second half of the short-rows are worked along the underside of the foot to the base of the toes.

Using a provisional method (see Glossary), CO 31 (39) sts. Work the first half and second half of the short-rows as for the toe-up sock heel until 1 wrapped st rem at each end of toe sts.

NEXT RND: With RS facing, sl 1 pwise wyb, knit to wrapped st, knit wrap tog with wrapped st, carefully remove provisional CO and place 31 (39) sts from CO on instep needle(s), knit across 31 (39) instep sts, knit wrap at start of toe sts tog with wrapped st, knit to end of toe sts—62 (78) sts total.

NEXT RND: Work instep sts as k1, k1f&b (see Glossary), k26 (34), k1f&b, k2; knit to end of heel sts—64 (80) sts total.

Divide sts (see Notes) as 33 (41) instep sts and 31 (39) heel sts if they are not already arranged this way. Rnds beg at side of foot, at start of instep sts.

FOOT

NEXT RND: Work Rnd 1 of Instep chart for your size over across 33 (41) instep sts, knit to end of rnd.

Working 33 (41) instep sts in chart patt as established and heel sts in St st, work even until foot measures 2 (2½)" (5 [6.5] cm) less than desired finished length from tip of toe to back of heel, ending with Rnd 6 of Instep chart.

HEEL

Work Rnd 7 of Instep chart for your size over 33 (41) instep sts, but do not work heel sts.

note: If using dpns, place all heel sts on a single needle.

The heel is worked using short-rows on the rem 31 (39) heel sts at end of rnd. Work the first half and second half of the short-rows as for the toe-up sock heel until 1 wrapped st rem at each end of toe sts.

NEXT ROW: (RS) Sl 1 pwise wyb, knit to last wrapped st, knit wrap tog with wrapped st, do not turn.

note: If using dpns, divide the heel sts on 2 dpns again.

NEXT RND: With RS still facing, work Rnd 8 of Instep chart for your size over 33 (41) instep sts, knit wrap at start of heel sts tog with wrapped st, knit to end of heel sts—64 (80) sts total.

LEG

Change to working all sts in patt from Leg chart for your size, working the 16 (20)-st patt rep 4 times for each rnd. Work even in patt until piece measures about 5" (12.5 cm) from top of heel for both sizes, or about 1" (2.5 cm) less than desired length to top of cuff ending with Rnd 8 of chart.

CUFF

RIB RND: *P1, k1; rep from * to end.

Rep last rnd until ribbed cuff measures 1" (2.5 cm). BO all sts as foll: K1, *yo, k1, pass the second and third sts on right needle (the first k1 and yo after it) over the first st on right needle; rep from * until 1 st rem, cut yarn, and fasten off.

FINISHING

Weave in loose ends. Block lightly.

caret + chevron socks

Speed Bump **SOCKS**

by **Deb Barnhill**

Self-striping yarns are the "comfort food" of sock knitting. Alternating stripes of bright stockinette and subdued gray ribbing are produced by letting the yarn lead the way. Simple but addictive, these combine the ease of a self-striping yarn with a bit of added polish.

FINISHED SIZE About 6 (7¼, 7¾)" (15 [18.5, 19.5] cm) foot circumference, 7 (8, 9¾)" (18 [20.5, 25] cm) foot length from back of heel to tip of toe and 6 (7¼, 7¾)" (15 [18.5, 19.5] cm) leg circumference. Foot length is adjustable. Socks shown measure 7¾" (19.5 cm) foot circumference.

YARN Fingering weight (Super Fine #1). *Shown here:* Patons Kroy Socks Ragg Shades (75% wool, 25% nylon; 166 yd [152 m]/50 g): #55102 blue striped ragg, 2 (2, 3) balls. Yarn distributed by Spinrite Yarns.

NEEDLES U.S. size 1 (2.25 mm): set of five double-pointed (dpn), two circular (cir), or one long cir. *Adjust needle size if necessary to obtain the correct gauge.*

NOTIONS 2 markers (m); stitch holder; tapestry needle.

GAUGE 34 sts and 48 rnds = 4" (10 cm) in St st.

stitch guide

SPEED BUMPS FOR LEG

At beg of a solid-color stripe, work in
St st. Knit to end of color stripe, then knit
an additional full rnd in the ragg color.
Work in k1, p1 rib at the beg of the second full rnd of the ragg color, regardless
of your position in the rnd. Cont in rib
to end of ragg color. Rep solid and ragg
stripes for desired leg length.

SPEED BUMPS FOR GUSSETS
AND FOOT

Throughout gussets and foot, the sole
of the sock is worked in St st and gusset
dec's are worked as indicated in patt.
For the instep, at the beg of a solid
color stripe, work in St st. Knit to end of
color stripe, then knit an additional full
rnd in the ragg color. Work in k1, p1 rib
at the beg of the second rnd of the ragg
color, regardless of your position in the
rnd (always keeping sole sts in St st),
and cont in rib to end of ragg color.
Depending on where the color change
falls, you may need to change st patt
partway across top of foot. Rep solid
and ragg stripes for desired length.

notes

* To accommodate different methods of
working—double-pointed needles, two
circulars, or one long circular—the stitches
are divided into two halves, which are
referred to as "instep" and "heel" stitches.
"Instep" stitches cover the top of the foot
and the front of the leg; these stitches are
on the first of two double-pointed needles,
first of two circular needles, or first half of
one long circular needle. "Heel" stitches
cover the bottom of the foot, the heel, and
the back of the leg; these stitches are on
the last two double-pointed needles, the
second of two circular needles, or second
half of one long circular needle.

* This pattern is written in the round with
markers, with the choice of needles left to
the knitter.

* For consistency, this pattern refers to the
color repeat in the yarn shown. "Solid"
refers to the brightly colored stripes
worked in stockinette. "Ragg" refers to the
heathered gray stripes worked in rib. If
you choose to substitute yarns, be sure to
choose one with stripe segments at least 3
rounds long at your chosen gauge and size.

* As a general rule, you should purl only
when the color of the working yarn is the
same color as the stitch you are working
into so that there are no color blips.

Cuff

At beg of a ragg stripe, CO 56 (64, 72) sts. Divide sts
and join for working in the rnd. Work in k1, p1 rib
for about 1½ (1½, 2)" (3.8 [3.8, 5] cm), or desired cuff
length, ending after completing a ragg stripe.

Leg

Change to speed bumps patt for leg (see Stitch Guide)
and work until leg measures about 5¾ (6½, 8½)" (14.5
[16.5, 21.5] cm) from CO, or desired length, ending after
completing a ragg stripe. Knit 1 rnd in next solid color.

Set aside working yarn but do not break yarn. A separate ball will be used to work the heel flap so the stripe sequence will continue down the foot without disruption.

Heel

HEEL FLAP

Place last 28 (32, 36) sts worked onto holder for top of foot. Heel flap will be worked back and forth over rem 28 (32, 36) sts.

With a second ball of yarn, wind to beg of same color stripe worked in last rnd of leg. Work heel flap with this ball as foll:

ROW 1: (RS) *Sl 1 purlwise (pwise) with yarn in back (wyb), k1; rep from * to end.

ROW 2: (WS) Sl 1 pwise with yarn in front (wyf), purl to end.

Rep last 2 rows 15 (17, 19) more times—heel flap measures about 1¾ (2, 2¼)" (4.5 [5, 5.5] cm).

TURN HEEL

Work short-rows as foll:

SHORT-ROW 1: (RS) Sl 1 pwise wyb, k16 (18, 20), ssk, k1, turn work.

SHORT-ROW 2: (WS) Sl 1 pwise wyf, p7, p2tog, p1, turn.

SHORT-ROW 3: (RS) Sl 1 pwise wyb, knit to 1 st before gap formed by previous row, ssk (1 st each side of gap), k1, turn.

SHORT-ROW 4: (WS) Sl 1 pwise wyf, purl to 1 st before gap formed by previous row, p2tog (1 st each side of gap), p1, turn.

Rep last 2 short-rows 3 (4, 5) more times, ending with a WS row—18 (20, 22) heel sts rem. Break heel flap yarn.

SHAPE GUSSETS

Place marker (pm) to indicate end of instep. With working yarn and RS facing, pick up and knit (see Glossary) 1 st between heel flap and leg, then 16 (18, 20) sts along edge of heel flap, k18 (20, 22) heel flap sts, pick up and knit 16 (18, 20) sts along edge of heel flap, then 1 st between heel flap and leg—80 (90, 100) sts total: 28 (32, 36) sts for instep, 52 (58, 64) sts for sole. Pm and rejoin for working in rnds as foll:

RND 1: (dec rnd) Work in speed bumps patt for gussets and foot (see Stitch Guide) to m, ssk, knit to last 2 sts, k2tog—2 sts dec'd.

RND 2: Work in speed bumps patt for gussets and foot to m, knit to end of rnd.

Rep last 2 rnds 11 (12, 13) more times—56 (64, 72) sts rem: 28 (32, 36) sts each for instep and sole.

Foot

Cont in patt as established until foot measures about 5½ (6½, 7¾)" (14 [16.5, 19.5] cm) from back of heel, or 1½ (1½, 2)" (3.8 [3.8, 5] cm) less than desired finished length, ending at the end a ragg stripe, then working a full rnd in the next solid stripe. Before beg the toe, every st on the needles should be a solid color.

Toe

note: Work all sts in St st.

RND 1: (dec rnd) *K1, ssk, knit to 3 sts before m, k2tog, k1; rep from * once more—4 sts dec'd.

RND 2: Knit.

Rep last 2 rnds 7 (8, 10) more times, then work Rnd 1 once more—20 (24, 24) sts rem; 10 (12, 12) sts each for instep and sole. Remove m and cut yarn, leaving a 12" (30.5 cm) tail.

Finishing

With tail threaded on a tapestry needle, use Kitchener st (see Glossary) to graft rem sts tog. Weave in loose ends and block lightly.

Flutterby SOCKS

by **Cat Bordhi**

Inspired as ever by nature, Cat Bordhi chose a slip-stitch pattern that reminded her of her grandson's delight at butterflies. Directions are provided to knit the socks toe-up or top-down.

FINISHED SIZE About 6 (7, 8)" (15 [18, 20.5] cm) foot circumference. Foot and leg lengths are adjustable. Socks shown measure 8" (20.5 cm) foot circumference.

Note: To allow for stretch, sock circumference measures about 15% smaller than actual circumference measured just above ball of foot (below).

foot circumference

YARN Fingering weight (#1 Super Fine). *Shown here:* Frog Tree Pediboo (80% merino, 20% bamboo; 255 yd [233 m]/100 g): 1164 blue (MC) and 1196 light blue (CC), 1 skein each.

NEEDLES U.S. size 1½ (2.5 mm): one long circular (cir), two cir, or set of four double-pointed (dpn). *Adjust needle size if necessary to obtain the correct gauge.*

Note: If using dpns, you will need a cir needle to try on the heel for fit.

NOTIONS Four locking markers (m) labeled A, B, C, D; tapestry needle.

GAUGE 32 sts and 50 rnds = 4" (10 cm) in St st.

stitch guide

FLUTTERBY

Dip right needle beneath all 3 horizontal strands (e.g. under Rnd 1 strand, then Rnd 3 strand, then Rnd 5 strand) so that needle tip emerges at top to grab a loop of yarn and bring it back down under all 3 strands, so that the loop pulls the 3 strands up. Slip next st as if to knit, insert left needle into fronts of these 2 sts (as if to ssk), and work them tog.

INSTEP PATTERN

(chart on page 32) Worked over 5 sts

RNDS 1, 3, AND 5: K1tbl, slip next 3 sts purlwise (pwise) with yarn in front (wyf), k1tbl.

RNDS 2, 4, AND 6: K1tbl, k3, k1tbl.

RNDS 7–9: Knit.

RNDS 10, 12, AND 14: K1tbl, slip next 3 sts pwise wyf, k1tbl.

RNDS 11 AND 13: K1tbl, k3, k1tbl.

RND 15: K1tbl, k1, Flutterby (see Stitch Guide), k1, k1tbl.

RNDS 16–18: Knit. Rep Rnds 1–18 for patt.

LEG PATTERN

(chart on page 32)

RNDS 1, 3, AND 5: *K1tbl, slip next 3 sts pwise wyf, k1tbl, k3 (2, 3); rep from * to D.

RNDS 2 AND 4: *K1tbl, k3, k1tbl, k3 (2, 3); rep from * to D.

RND 6: *K1tbl, k3, k1tbl, k3 (2, 3), k1tbl, k1, Flutterby, k1, k1tbl, k3 (2, 3); rep from * to D.

RNDS 7–9: Knit.

RNDS 10, 12, AND 14: *K1tbl, slip next 3 sts pwise wyf, k1tbl, k3 (2, 3); rep from * to D.

RNDS 11 AND 13: *K1tbl, k3, k1tbl, k3 (2, 3); rep from * to D.

RND 15: *K1tbl, k1, Flutterby, k1, k1tbl, k3 (2, 3), k1tbl, k3, k1tbl, k3 (2, 3); rep from * to D.

RNDS 16–18: Knit. Rep Rnds 1–18 for patt.

Watch Cat demonstrate elements of this pattern in the following videos:

WORKING WITH 1 LONG CIR
http://tinyurl.com/3hyg7zw

WORKING WITH 2 CIR
http://tinyurl.com/6xh63s2

WORKING WITH DPNS
http://tinyurl.com/322j6ob

SWEET TOMATO HEEL
http://tinyurl.com/4x4xmp2

JENY'S SURPRISINGLY STRETCHY BIND-OFF
http://tinyurl.com/3z6haza

Toe-Up Version

TOE

With MC, work Turkish CO as foll: Hold 2 needles parallel with points aimed to the right. Leaving a 10" (25.5 cm) tail, make a slipknot and place on lower needle. Wrap working yarn under, around, and over both needles (like a wave receding under the needles, then coming over the needles toward you) 3 times. Begin a fourth wrap but stop just before coming over the needles, securing the working yarn against the needle with a finger. Use the working yarn to knit 3 sts from top needle. With RS facing, rotate needles clockwise 180 degrees, remove slipknot from needle, and pull knot free.

RND 1: Knit 6 sts (3 on each needle) with tail and working yarn held together—6 doubled sts; 12 loops on needles. Drop tail yarn and continue with working yarn alone.

RND 2: Knit into each half of doubled sts—12 sts.

note: If using dpns, place 4 sts on each of 3 needles.

RND 3: Place marker C for beg of rnd (or use intersection to represent C), [k1, k1f&b (see Glossary)] 6 times—18 sts.

RND 4: Knit.

RND 5: [K2, k1f&b] 6 times—24 sts.

RND 6: Knit.

RND 7: [K3, k1f&b] 6 times—30 sts.

RND 8: Knit.

RND 9: [K4, k1f&b] 6 times—36 sts.

RNDS 10–11: Knit.

RND 12: [K5, k1f&b] 6 times—42 sts.

RNDS 13–14: Knit.

RND 15: [K6, k1f&b] 6 times—48 sts. Cont for your size as foll:

Size 6" (15 cm) only

Skip to Foot.

Sizes 7 (8)" (18 [20.5] cm) only

RNDS 16–17: Knit.

RND 18: [K7, k1f&b] 6 times—54 sts.

RNDS 19–20: Knit. Cont for your size as foll:

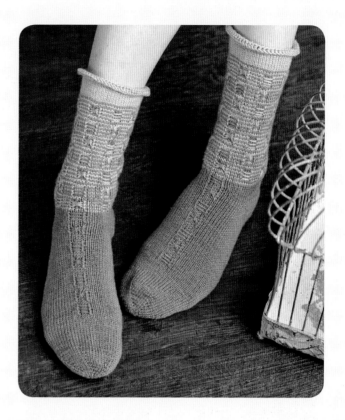

Size 7" (18 cm) only

RND 21: [K26, k1f&b] twice—56 sts.

Skip to Foot.

Size 8" (20.5 cm) only

RND 21: [K8, k1f&b] 6 times—60 sts.

RNDS 22–23: Knit.

RND 24: [K9, k1f&b, k9, k1f&b, k10] 2 times—64 sts.

FOOT

note: First 24 (28, 32) sts will be worked for sole. Knit until toe measures about 3" (7.5 cm) long.

NEXT RND: K34 (40, 46), place marker D, knit to C (end of rnd).

Begin Flutterby patt as foll:

NEXT RND: Knit to D, work Instep chart (see Stitch Guide or chart on page 32), knit to C.

Work in pattern until sock reaches "hinge" at top of instep where leg and foot bend (**Figure 1, page 32**), stopping at any rnd that brings you to the hinge; note last rnd worked so you will know where to resume.

Instep

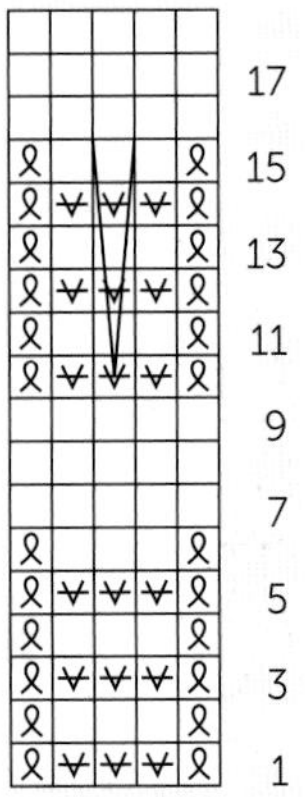
17
15
13
11
9
7
5
3
1

Leg

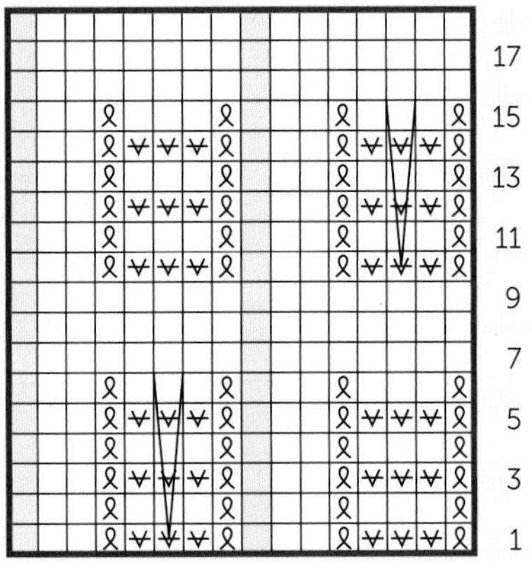
17
15
13
11
9
7
5
3
1

16 (14, 16)-st repeat

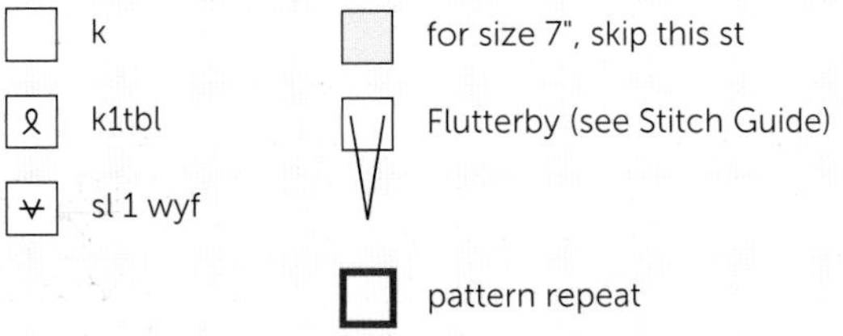
k
k1tbl
sl 1 wyf
for size 7", skip this st
Flutterby (see Stitch Guide)
pattern repeat

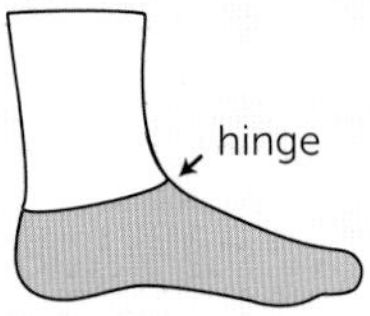
hinge

FIGURE 1

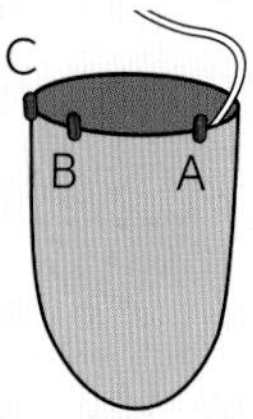
C
B
A

FIGURE 2

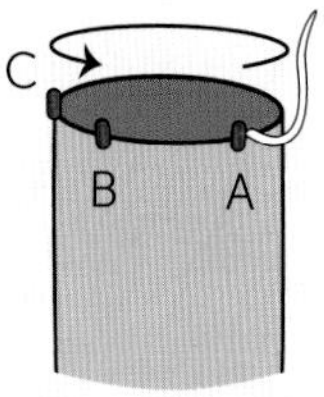
C
B
A

FIGURE 3

notes

- Always slip first stitch of each row purlwise with yarn held to front if on purl side or to back if on knit side; this keeps the yarn out of the way.
- Keep strong tension on first few stitches of each row for best results.
- Marker C can be removed if desired.
- All wedges begin at A.

Heel Set-up

The heel is worked on about ⅔ of the total sts, with the remaining ⅓ centered on the instep.

NEXT RND: Knit to 6 (7, 8) sts before D and place marker A. Without knitting further, place marker B 11 (12, 13) sts after D—17 (19, 21) front/instep sts (from A to B), 31 (37, 43) back heel sts (from B to C to A). Yarn waits at A.

Arrange Front and Back

note: Intersections can replace stitch markers if desired.

Arrange sts as follows **(Figure 2)**:

DPNS: Sts for instep on 1 needle; sts for heel on 2 needles.

2 CIRCULARS: Front and back on separate needles.

1 CIRCULAR: Front and back on separate cable sections.

SWEET TOMATO HEEL

Unlike the standard short-row heel, which has two wedges with steep sides, a Sweet Tomato Heel has three wedges with gently sloping sides. After each wedge is complete, two full rounds anchor and integrate it with the instep. The heel is custom fitted by either ending the third wedge early (for a small heel) or completing it (for a larger heel).

Begin Wedge

Slide marker A to right needle, turn work.

SHORT-ROW 1: (WS) Slip 1, purl to B, turn **(Figure 3)**.

note: From this point forward, each row will be 2 sts shorter than the previous row.

SHORT-ROW 2: (RS) Slip 1, knit to 2 sts before A, turn.

SHORT-ROW 3: Slip 1, purl to 2 sts before B, turn.

SHORT-ROW 4: Slip 1, knit to 4 sts before A, turn.

SHORT-ROW 5: Slip 1, purl to 4 sts before B, turn.

SHORT-ROW 6: Slip 1, knit to 6 sts before A, turn.

SHORT-ROW 7: Slip 1, purl to 6 sts before B, turn.

SHORT-ROW 8: Slip 1, knit to 8 sts before A, turn.

SHORT-ROW 9: Slip 1, purl to 8 sts before B, turn.

Continue working shorter rows until, as you begin a knit row, the center of the heel (between wrapped sts) measures about 1" (2.5 cm) wide.

WEDGE IN PROGRESS

Markers A and B mark start and end of heel. Slip stitches (in blue) begin each row. A pair of stitches—a slip stitch followed by a knit stitch—is located above each gap. Paired stitches, separated by gaps, begin to line up on the sides (see below). Always turn 2 stitches before the next gap.

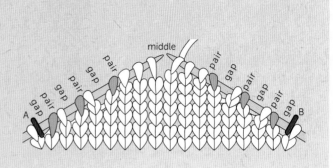

NEXT RND: (RS; Thanks-Ma Rnd) Slip 1, knit the center of the heel to the last stitch before the first gap (**Figure 4**), work the Thanks-Ma Rnd as described and illustrated on page 34.

Work [k1, Thanks-Ma] "downhill" to A, work in pattern around the front of the sock to B (keeping center 5 sts of instep in pattern following Instep chart).

On the "uphill" side, a gap appears between B and Blue (**Figures 5 and 6**). Ma's arm bridges the gap. Ma's right side may be hiding behind her left side; don't let her fool you.

Find Ma's right side and work a Thanks-Ma to close the gap. Work [k1, Thanks-Ma] uphill until all gaps are closed. Knit across the middle, then downhill to A.

NEXT RND: Work even in pattern to A.

First wedge is complete (anchored and integrated by full rounds).

Work second wedge following the same instructions as first wedge, ending with the second full round and keeping center 5 instep sts in pattern following Instep chart.

Work a third wedge until the center of the heel is about 2" (5 cm) wide, ending after a purl row. Try on the sock for fit; if using dpns, slip sts onto a circular needle to try on. For many knitters, working only part of a third wedge is sufficient; if so, skip to Heel Completion. If not, continue wedge directions and work more short-rows (each one 2 sts shorter than previous row) until heel top and instep top are about even and fit matches (**Figure 7, page 35**), ending after completing a purl row.

Heel Completion

Knit across the center of the heel to the last stitch before the first gap, work a Thanks-Ma, work [k1, Thanks-Ma] to A, remove A, work around the front of the sock in pattern (keeping center 5 sts of instep in pattern following Instep chart), remove B, work [Thanks-Ma, k1] until all gaps are closed.

gap

FIGURE 4

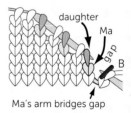

daughter

Ma

B

Ma's arm bridges gap

FIGURE 5

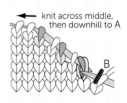

knit across middle, then downhill to A

B

FIGURE 6

flutterby socks

THE THANKS-MA ROUND

Daughter Blue rises from her yellow Ma. See how Ma's yellow arm bridges the gap? Lifting Ma up onto the needle will shorten her arm and close the gap.

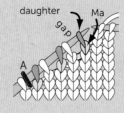

TO WORK A THANKS-MA

Lift Ma's right side up onto the needle in front of Blue. Knit them together (as if to knit 2 together), and the gap closes. Thanks, Ma!

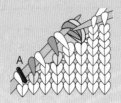

LEG

Knit to D; this is new beg of rnd. The pattern will now circle the entire leg and be worked in stripes. Work in pattern to the end of Rnd 7 or 16 (whichever comes first). Beg with next rnd of patt, work 65 rnds according to Leg chart (see Stitch Guide or chart) over all sts, alternating 1 rnd CC then 1 rnd MC throughout, ending with Rnd 9 or 18. Break C and cont in MC.

note: Always pick up the new color from beneath the old. The pattern (particularly the twisted stitches) makes it difficult to see the color change, so the yarn change can fall in front without being seen.

CUFF

With CC, work in stockinette stitch for 1¼" (3.2 cm). Use Jeny's Surprisingly Stretchy method (see Glossary) or another elastic method to BO all sts.

Weave in loose ends.

Top-Down Version

CUFF

With CC, loosely CO 48 (56, 64) sts. Place marker D for beg of rnd and join for working in rnds, being careful not to twist sts.

Knit for 1¼" (3.2 cm).

LEG

Leg is worked in stripes. Change colors at D every rnd, always picking up the new color from beneath the old. The pattern (particularly the twisted stitches) makes it difficult to see the color change, so the yarn change can fall in front without being seen.

Knit 1 rnd with MC; knit 1 rnd with CC; knit 1 rnd with MC.

Changing colors at D every round, work Leg chart in the rnd over all stitches 3 times, then work Rnds 1–7 once more. Break CC.

HEEL SET-UP

Work Heel Set-up as for Toe-Up Version.

SWEET TOMATO HEEL

Work Sweet Tomato Heel as for Toe-Up Version through Heel Completion, keeping first 5 sts after D in patt following Instep chart for heel full rnds.

✳ TIP

Cat's advice: Try the sock on as you go! Work increases and decreases as needed to fit your foot, and work them where they're needed.

FIGURE 7   FIGURE 8

note: You will not be using marker C. End third wedge when ankle (see bold line in Figure 8) is level and side of heel is just shy of perpendicular.

The next rnd is Rnd 13.

FOOT

Work evenly around the foot, maintaining the first 5 sts after D in pattern following Instep chart until foot measures about 3" (7.5 cm) less than desired length to toe, ending after Rnd 6 or 15 is completed, then change to stockinette st.

TOE

Count the sts in 1 vertical inch (row gauge) and divide that number into 13 (19, 22), which is the number of rounds your toe will use, minus the final 2, which do not add length. The answer equals the length of your toe. Continue working even in the round until the foot measures the desired finished length minus the toe length.

Size 7" (18 cm) only

NEXT RND: [K26, k2tog] 2 times—54 sts rem.

Work 2 rnds even.

Size 8" (20.5 cm) only

NEXT RND: [K9, k2tog, k9, k2tog, k10] 2 times—60 sts rem.

Work 2 rnds even.

All sizes

Arrange sts as follows:

CIRCULAR(S): One half of the number of sts on each needle or cable section.

DPNS: One third of the number of sts on each of 3 needles.

Place markers every 8 (9, 10) sts (intersections may represent some markers).

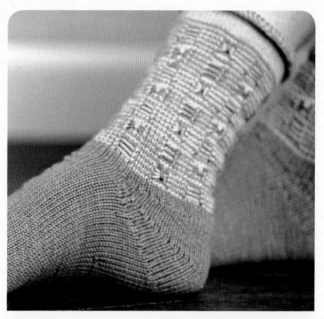

Begin toe decreases:

RND 1: [Knit to 2 sts before marker, k2tog] 6 times—6 sts dec'd.

RNDS 2–3: Knit.

Repeat Rnds 1–3 two (three, four) more times—30 sts remain. Rep Rnds 1–2 two more times—18 sts remain. Repeat Rnd 1 twice—6 sts remain.

Break yarn, leaving an 8" (20.5 cm) tail. Draw tail through remaining 6 sts, pull tight, and weave in all ends.

get your cast-on!

by **Karen Frisa**

Get your next pair of toe-up socks off on the right foot with one of these four cast-ons

Maybe you like to use every yard of sock yarn. Perhaps you want to try on your socks as you go. Or it could be that the Kitchener stitch gives you hives.

There are plenty of reasons to knit socks from the toe up. Try each of these four methods to find your favorite fit.

Turkish/Eastern

Turkish/Eastern

This super-simple invisible method can double as a provisional cast-on.

1 Hold two needles (dpns, 2 cir needles, or both ends of 1 cir) parallel. Leaving a 6" (12.5 cm) tail in front, bring yarn from front to back between needles. *Wrap working yarn over top of both needles, around front, and under needles to back. Rep from * until number of wraps over top needle equals half the number of stitches needed. Make sure that you have the same number of wraps on bottom needle (**Figure 1**).

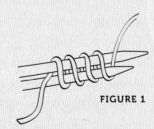

FIGURE 1

For dpns only: Use a third needle to work across the top.

For 2 cir needles only: Pull out bottom needle so that stitches that were on that needle rest on the cable. Drop bottom cir and work across top stitches with only top cir needle.

For 1 cir needle only: Pull out the bottom needle so that the stitches that were on that needle rest on the cable, being careful not to pull stitches off needle altogether. Use bottom needle to work across top stitches.

2 Work stitches on top needle; stitches should be seated so that right leg is in front **(Figure 2)**. Note that last stitch is anchored only by the tail; be careful not to pull free **(Figure 3)**.

For dpns only: Rotate needles so that you are ready to work across stitches that were cast onto bottom needle. Use needle just emptied to work across the bottom.

For 2 cir needles only: Drop top cir and rotate work so that you are ready to work across stitches cast onto bottom needle. Move stitches from cable to tip of needle ready to work.

For 1 cir needle only: Slide stitches just worked from tip of the needle to cable. Slide stitches that were held on cable to tip of the needle ready to work.

3 With the bottom needle now on top, work the stitches on this needle **(Figure 4)**. Working with dpns, divide the stitches on the original top needle between two needles for ease of working **(Figure 5)**.

4 Continue working in the round, increasing as called for in pattern until full circumference is achieved.

VARIATION

Figure-Eight Cast-On

Begin as for Turkish cast-on, with needles held together and tail at the front. *Bring yarn over top needle, then between the needles to the back, behind and under bottom needle to front, and again between needles to back. Rep from * until the number of wraps over the top needle equals half the number of stitches needed. Make sure that you have the same number of wraps on bottom needle; yarn is at back **(Figure 6)**.

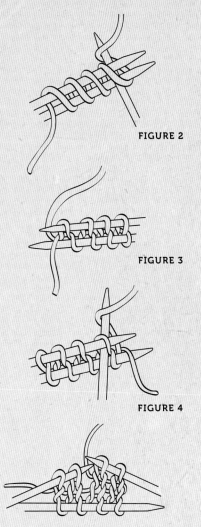

FIGURE 2

FIGURE 3

FIGURE 4

FIGURE 5

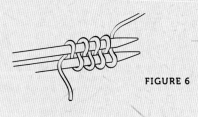

FIGURE 6

Work across top needle as for Turkish cast-on. When you rotate needles to work across bottom stitches, left legs of stitches will be seated in front of needle. Work through back loops to correct mount.

Square Toe

This unusual cast-on wraps around the toes from side to side. Adjust the number of stitches to meet your needs.

Square Toe

1 Provisionally cast on four stitches. Beginning with a RS row, work eight rows in stockinette stitch (**Figure 1**).

2 Knit one row; do not turn. Rotate work 90° clockwise. With a spare needle, pick up and knit six stitches along left edge (**Figure 2**).

3 Rotate work 90° clockwise again, then knit across provisionally cast-on stitches. Rotate work 90° clockwise again and pick up and knit six stitches along right edge (**Figure 3**)—twenty stitches.

4 To shape toe, increase one stitch from each end of the top and bottom needles (the needles with four stitches); round begins at center top of square (between third and fourth stitches of Needle 1). Rearrange stitches on needles as needed.

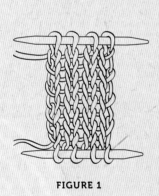

FIGURE 1

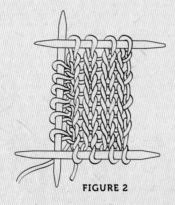

FIGURE 2

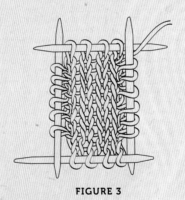

FIGURE 3

Circular

A rosebud closure worked in reverse, this cast-on is the perfect way to start a star or three-pointed toe.

Circular

1 Holding tail between ring and pinkie fingers, wrap working yarn counterclockwise around thumb and grasp working yarn between forefinger and ring finger **(Figure 1)**.

2 Dip needle down into loop around thumb, up and over working yarn, and back out of thumb loop, drawing up a stitch on needle **(Figure 2)**.

3 Wrap working yarn around needle to make a yarnover **(Figure 3)**.

4 Repeat Steps 2 and 3 until you have cast on one fewer stitch than you need, then repeat Step 2 once more **(Figure 4)**.

5 Distribute stitches over dpns and work in the round, increasing as directed in pattern. Pull tail tight to snug center ring and weave in tail.

 TIP

This cast-on creates an odd number of stitches; for an even number, either cast on one fewer stitch and increase in the first round or cast on one stitch more and decrease in the first round.

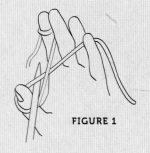

FIGURE 1

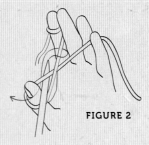

FIGURE 2

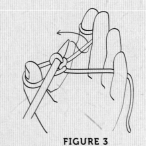

FIGURE 3

FIGURE 4

get your cast-on!

Short-Row Toe

This cast-on is worked just like its cousin, the short-row heel. If working in garter stitch, skip the step of picking up wraps.

Short-row Toe

1 Provisionally cast on half the number of stitches needed for foot circumference.

2 **SHORT-ROW ON RS:** Work to one stitch before turning point. Slip next stitch to right needle purlwise **(Figure 1)**. Bring yarn to RS, slip stitch back to left needle, and bring yarn to WS **(Figure 2)**. Turn work.

3 **SHORT-ROW ON WS:** Work to one stitch before turning point. Bring yarn to RS **(Figure 3)**. Slip stitch back to left needle and bring yarn to WS **(Figure 4)**. Turn work.

4 Repeat Steps 2 and 3, wrapping one stitch before wrapped stitch from last row, until about one-third of stitches are unwrapped with about one-third of stitches wrapped on each side **(Figure 5)**. End after working short-row on WS.

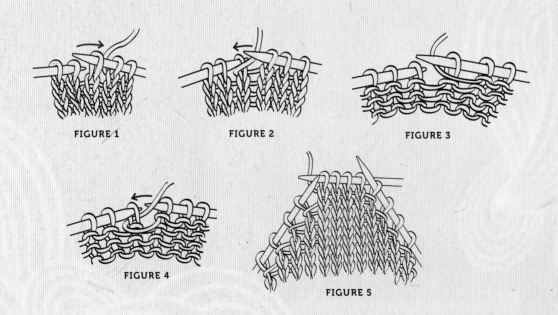

FIGURE 1   **FIGURE 2**   **FIGURE 3**

FIGURE 4

FIGURE 5

5 **DOUBLE-WRAP ROW ON RS:** Work to first stitch wrapped on last RS row. With right needle, scoop RS portion of wrap(s) onto left needle and knit it together with its stitch (**Figure 6**). Slip next stitch to right needle purlwise, wrap and turn.

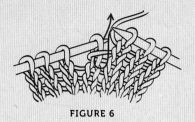

FIGURE 6

6 **DOUBLE-WRAP ROW ON WS:** Work to first stitch wrapped on last WS row. With right needle, scoop RS portion of wrap(s) onto left needle (**Figure 7**) and purl it together with its stitch. Slip next stitch to right needle purlwise, wrap and turn.

7 Repeat Steps 5 and 6, picking up double-wrapped stitch from last row and double-wrapping next stitch, until one double-wrapped stitch remains at each end of row. End after double-wrapping last stitch of WS row.

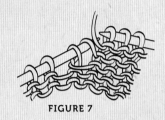

FIGURE 7

8 Work to last stitch of RS row. Scoop wraps onto needle and work them with last stitch. Work across all provisionally cast-on stitches. On next round, first stitch will be double-wrapped from last WS row. With right needle, scoop up RS portion of wraps and slip wrapped stitch to right needle along with wraps. Knit wraps together with stitch through back loops (**Figure 8**). Work foot in pattern.

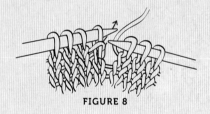

FIGURE 8

Oak + Acorn SOCKS

by **SpillyJane**

For Jane Dupuis, growing up in a house that was not much older than she was—a house that "held no secrets"—was nearly unbearable. The house's saving grace was the massive oak tree that was planted long ago to mark the boundary of a long-lost farmer's field. These socks are Jane's ode to that tree.

FINISHED SIZE About 8 (10¼)" (20.5 [26] cm) foot circumference. Foot length is adjustable. Socks shown measure 8" (20.5 cm) in foot circumference.

YARN Fingering weight (Super Fine #1) or Sportweight (Fine #2). *Shown here:* Smaller socks: Louet Gems Fingering Weight (100% merino; 185 yd [169 m]/50 g): #36 linen grey (MC), 2 skeins; #53 caribou (CC1, dark brown), #47 terra cotta (CC2), and #44 sandalwood (CC3, medium brown), 1 skein each. Larger socks: Louet Gems Sport Weight (100% merino wool; 225 yd [205 m]/100 g): #36 linen grey (MC), 2 skeins; #53 caribou (CC1, dark brown), #47 terra cotta (CC2), and #44 sandalwood (CC3, medium brown), 1 skein each.

Note: Depending on gauge and the desired length of the sock, you may use very little if any of the second skein of MC.

NEEDLES *Smaller socks:* U.S. size 1 (2.25 mm): set of five double-pointed (dpn). *Larger socks:* U.S. size 2 (2.75 mm): set of five double-pointed (dpn). *Adjust needle sizes if necessary to obtain the correct gauge.*

NOTIONS Markers (m); waste yarn for holders; tapestry needle.

GAUGE *Smaller socks:* 18 and 24 rnds = 2" (5 cm) in solid-color St st. *Larger socks:* 14 sts and 20 rnds = 2" (5 cm) in solid-color St st.

notes

✖ If there is only a single number given in the directions, it applies to both sizes. When there are two numbers, the first applies to the smaller fingering weight socks, and the second number (in parentheses) applies to the larger sportweight socks.

✖ Slip stitches to waste yarn and try on the socks frequently while working the chart. Some knitters work stranded colorwork more tightly than stockinette, which may make the socks too small to fit over the heel. If necessary, use a larger needle size for the colorwork portion of the leg to maintain the correct gauge.

Cuff

With MC, loosely CO 72 sts and divide evenly over 4 dpn. Being careful not to twist sts, sl first st from Needle 1 to Needle 4 and pass last CO st from Needle 4 over the sl st and onto Needle 1 to join in the rnd. Place marker (pm) for beg of rnd.

RIB RND: *K2 through back loops (tbl), p2; rep from * to end of rnd.

Rep the rib rnd 9 more times. Change to St st, and knit 2 rnds.

Leg

Work Rnds 1–39 of Oak + Acorn chart, working 36-st patt rep 2 times for each rnd, ending with Rnd 39.

note: For a longer leg, rep Rnds 37–39 of chart as many times as desired.

Heel

NEXT ROW: With MC, k36 onto a single dpn; place rem 36 sts on holder or divide on 2 dpn to work later for instep.

Heel is worked back and forth in rows over first 36 sts of rnd.

HEEL FLAP

NEXT ROW: (WS) Sl 1 purlwise (pwise) with yarn in front (pwise wyf), purl to end.

NEXT ROW: (RS) Sl 1 pwise with yarn in back (wyb), knit to end.

Rep last 2 rows until heel flap measures 2 (2¾)" (5 [7] cm) or desired length, ending with a WS row.

TURN HEEL

SHORT-ROW 1: (RS) Sl 1 pwise wyb, k20, ssk, k1, turn work.

SHORT-ROW 2: Sl 1 pwise wyf, p7, p2tog, p1, turn.

SHORT-ROW 3: Sl 1 pwise wyb, knit to 1 st before gap created on last row, ssk (1 st from each side of gap), k1, turn.

SHORT-ROW 4: Sl 1 pwise wyf, purl to 1 st before gap created on last row, p2tog (1 st from each side of gap), p1, turn.

Rep Short-rows 3 and 4 until all heel stitches have been worked, ending with WS Short-row 4—22 sts rem.

NEXT ROW: (RS) K11 heel sts to center of heel; this is now the beg of the rnd.

SHAPE GUSSETS

SET-UP RND: Using an empty dpn, k11 rem heel sts, pick up and knit (see Glossary) 1 st in each slipped st along edge of heel flap (working sts tbl to tighten), M1 (see Glossary) in gap between heel and instep—this is now Needle 1. Knit the 36 held instep sts onto 2 dpn—18 sts on each needle; these are now Needles 2 and 3. Using an empty dpn, M1 between instep and heel flap, then pick up and knit 1 st in each slipped st along edge of heel flap (working sts tbl to tighten) k11 heel sts—this is now Needle 4.

note: Your total stitch count and the number of sts on Needles 1 and 4 will vary depending on how many sts were picked up along the sides of your heel flap.

RND 1: (dec rnd) On Needle 1, knit to last 3 sts, k2tog, k1; on Needles 2 and 3, knit; on Needle 4, k1, ssk, knit to end—2 sts dec'd; 1 st each on Needles 1 and 4.

RND 2: Knit.

Rep Rnds 1 and 2 as many times as necessary until 72 sts rem.

Oak + Acorn

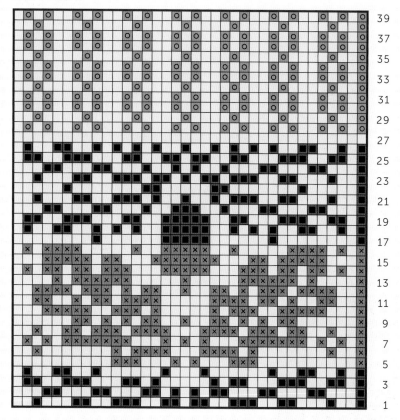

	MC
	CC1
	CC2
	CC3
	pattern repeat

Foot

Work in St st until piece measures about 2¼ (2¾)" (5.5 [7] cm) less than desired length from back of heel to tip of toe. If necessary, rearrange sts so that there are 18 sts on each dpn, with beg of rnd in center of sole.

Toe

RND 1: On Needle 1, knit to last 3 sts, k2tog, k1; on Needle 2, k1, ssk, knit to end; on Needle 3, knit to last 3 sts, k2tog, k1; on Needle 4, k1, ssk, knit to end—4 sts dec'd.

RND 2: Knit.

Rep the last 2 rnds 12 more times—20 sts rem; 5 sts on each needle. Knit the 5 sts from Needle 1 onto the end of Needle 4, then place sts from Needles 2 and 3 on same needle—10 sts each on 2 dpn.

Finishing

Use Kitchener st (see Glossary) to graft rem sts tog. Weave in loose ends. Block lightly if desired.

Twisted Diamonds
SOCKS

by **Ann Budd**

The twisted ribs in these socks flow seamlessly from picots in the Channel Island cast-on. With the picots aligned with knit stitches in the k1, p1 rib, this decorative cast-on becomes almost invisible. Twisted knit stitches make the ribbing pop, and cables further twist the stitches into a diamond pattern. The cables near the top of the leg continue clock-fashion along the sides of the leg, where they separate at the heel.

FINISHED SIZE About 7¾ (8¾)" (19.5 [22] cm) foot circumference and 9½ (10¼)" (24 [26] cm) foot length from back of heel to tip to toe. Foot length is adjustable. Socks shown measure 7¾" (19.5 cm) foot circumference.

YARN Fingering weight (Super Fine #1). *Shown here:* Lana Grossa Meilenweit 50 Seta/Cashmere (65% merino, 15% silk, 16% polyamide, 4% cashmere; 208 yd [190 m]/50 g): #7 medium blue, 2 balls. Yarn distributed by Muench.

NEEDLES U.S. sizes 2 (2.75 mm) and 3 (3.25 mm): set of four double-pointed (dpn). *Adjust needle size if necessary to obtain the correct gauge.*

NOTIONS Markers (m); cable needle (cn); tapestry needle.

GAUGE 28 sts and 44 rnds = 4" (10 cm) in St st on smaller needles; 40 sts and 44 rnds = 4" (10 cm) in twisted rib on smaller needles, relaxed.

notes

✖ To work this pattern using two circular needles or the magic loop technique, place 32 (36) stitches on each needle/half of needle. When working the heel, rearrange stitches so that the heel flap stitches are on one needle/half of needle and the instep stitches are on the other. When picking up stitches for the gusset, pick up all stitches using the needle/half of needle that holds the heel stitches; beginning of round will be at center of this needle/half of needle.

✖ In gusset and toe shaping instructions, Needle 1 refers to the stitches from the beginning of round to the end of the first needle/half of needle, Needle 2 refers to all of the stitches on the second needle/half of needle, and Needle 3 refers to the stitches from the beginning of the first needle/half of needle to the beginning of round.

Leg

With larger needles and using the Channel Island method (see page 51) CO 65 (73) sts, including the initial slipknot. Arrange sts as foll: slipknot and 19 (23) sts on Needle 1, 24 sts on Needle 2, and 21 (25) sts on Needle 3. Join for working in the rnd by transferring the last st CO (on Needle 3) to first needle (in front of the slipknot), lift the slipknot up and over the last st CO and off the needle—64 (72) sts rem: 20 (24) sts each on Needles 1 and 3, 24 sts on Needle 2. Place marker (pm) for beg of rnd.

SET-UP RND: *K1tbl, p1; rep from * around.

Work in twisted rib for 13 more rnds—14 rnds total.

Work Rows 1–14 of Upper Leg chart once, then work Rows 1–7 once more—piece measures about 3½" (9 cm) from CO.

SET UP CLOCKS

Change to smaller needles and cont to work diamond patt along sides of leg as foll: Work 12 (14) sts in twisted rib, pm, beg with Row 1 (8) of chart, work 7 sts according to Diamond chart, pm, work 25 (29) sts in twisted rib, pm, beg with Row 1 (8) of chart, work 7 sts according to Diamond chart, pm, work 13 (15) sts in twisted rib. Cont as established until piece measures about 7 (7½)" (18 [19] cm) from CO or desired length to top of heel, ending with Rnd 1 or 8 of chart.

Heel

HEEL FLAP

Work 16 (18) sts in patt, turn work, sl 1, work 32 (36) sts in patt—33 (37) heel sts (heel sts beg and end with p1); rem 31 (35) sts will be worked later for instep. Working heel sts back and forth in rows, work Rows 1–8 of Heel Flap chart 4 times, then work Rows 1–4 zero (once) more—32 (36) rows total; 16 (18) chain sts along each selvedge edge.

TURN HEEL

ROW 1: (RS) K19 (21), ssk, k1, turn.

ROW 2: (WS) Sl 1, p6, p2tog, p1, turn.

ROW 3: Sl 1, knit to 1 st before gap, ssk (1 st from each side of gap), k1, turn.

ROW 4: Sl 1, purl to 1 st before gap, p2tog (1 st from each side of gap), p1, turn.

Rep Rows 3 and 4 four (five) more times—21 (23) heel sts rem.

NEXT ROW: (RS) Sl 1, knit to 1 st before gap, ssk, turn.

NEXT ROW: (WS) Sl 1, purl to 1 st before gap, p2tog, turn—19 (21) heel sts rem.

SHAPE GUSSETS

Rejoin for working in the rnd as foll:

RND 1: With an empty needle (Needle 1) and RS facing, k19 (21) heel sts, then pick up and knit 16 (18) sts along selvedge edge of heel flap (1 st in each chain selvedge st) and 1 st at base of heel flap (to help prevent a hole); with Needle 2, work 31 (35) instep sts according to Rnd 1 of Instep chart; with Needle 3, pick up and knit 1 st at base of heel flap (to help prevent a hole) and 16 (18) sts along selvedge edge (1 st in each chain selvedge st), then knit first 9 (10) heel sts again—84 (94) sts total: 27 (30) sts on Needle 1, 31 (35) instep sts on Needle 2, 26 (29) sts on Needle 3.

Rnd beg at center of heel sts.

RND 2: Needle 1: Knit to last 3 sts, k2tog, p1; Needle 2: Work 31 (35) instep sts according to Instep chart; Needle 3: P1, ssk, knit to end—2 sts dec'd.

RND 3: Work even in patt.

Rep Rnds 2 and 3 nine (ten) more times—64 (72) sts rem.

Foot

Cont in patt, working sole sts in St st and instep sts according to Instep chart, until piece measures about 7¾ (8)" (19.5 [20.5] cm) from back of heel, or about 1¾ (2¼)" (4.5 [5.5] cm) less than desired finished length.

Toe

Transfer last st on Needle 1 to instep needle (Needle 2)—16 (18) sole sts on Needle 1, 32 (36) instep sts on Needle 2, 16 (18) sole sts on Needle 3. Dec as foll:

RND 1: Needle 1: Knit to last 3 sts, k2tog, k1; Needle 2: K1, ssk, knit to last 3 sts, k2tog, k1; Needle 3: K1, ssk, knit to end—4 sts dec'd.

Diamond

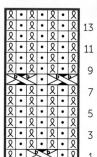

Heel Flap

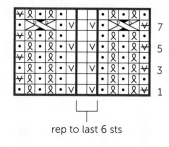

rep to last 6 sts

Upper Leg

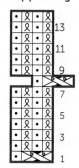

Instep

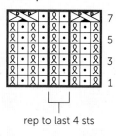

rep to last 4 sts

☐ k on RS; p on WS	ⱱ sl 1 wyf on RS; sl 1 wyb on WS
· p on RS; k on WS	⤬ sl 2 sts onto cn, hold in front, k1tbl, sl purl st from cn to left needle, p1, k1tbl from cn
ℓ k1tbl on RS; p1tbl on WS	
v sl 1 wyb on RS; sl 1 wyf on WS	☐ pattern repeat

RND 2: Knit.

Rep Rnds 1 and 2 seven (nine) more times—32 sts rem. Rep Rnd 1 only 4 times—16 sts rem: 4 sts on Needle 1, 8 sts on Needle 2, and 4 sts on Needle 3. With Needle 3, knit the sts on Needle 1—8 sts on each of 2 needles. Cut yarn, leaving a 12" (30.5 cm) tail.

Finishing

Graft toe with Kitchener st (see Glossary). Weave in loose ends, tightening up holes at gussets as necessary. Block lightly.

twisted diamonds socks

cast-ons **for comfy cuffs**

by **Karen Frisa**

The cast-on method can make or break your top-down socks. Not only can it add a nice decorative edge, but it can mean the difference between socks that go on easily and socks that don't! These four cast-on methods are attractive, elastic, and particularly good for socks.

Old Norwegian Cast-On

This variation of the long-tail cast-on has an attractive edge.

1   Make a slipknot and place it on the right needle. Hold the yarn and leave a tail as for the long-tail cast-on **(Figure 1)**. The slipknot counts as the first stitch.

2   Bring the needle in front of your thumb, under both strands around your thumb, down into the center of the thumb loop, then forward toward you. Next, bring the needle over the strand going to the index finger to grab it **(Figure 2)**.

3   Bring the needle back through the thumb loop on your thumb **(Figure 3)**, turning the thumb slightly to make room for the needle to pass through.

4   Drop the loop off your thumb **(Figure 4)** and, placing your thumb back in the V configuration, tighten up the resulting stitch on the needle.

Repeat Steps 2 through 4 for the desired number of stitches. Distribute the stitches over your chosen needles and join for working in the round.

PROS Very stretchy + can be worked fairly quickly + has nice edge

CONS Trickier to work than long-tail cast-on

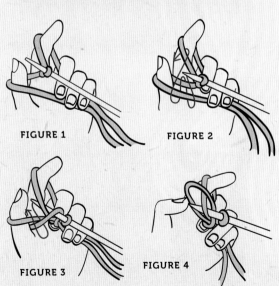

FIGURE 1

FIGURE 2

FIGURE 3

FIGURE 4

Channel Island Cast-On

This is a great cast-on for 1x1 ribbing that makes a pretty line of yarn "beads" along the edge.

1 Holding three strands of yarn together, make a slipknot about six inches from the ends and place it on the right needle (this does not count as a stitch). Divide the three strands, using a single strand as the working yarn and the two remaining strands as the tail.

2 Place the single strand around your index finger. Wrap the two-strand tail counterclockwise around your thumb so that two wraps are visible below your thumbnail. Make a yarnover on the needle with the single strand (**Figure 1**).

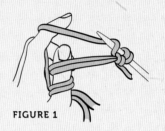

FIGURE 1

3 Beginning at the base of your thumb, slide the needle up through both thumb loops, then over the single strand going to your index finger to grab it, then go back down through the two thumb loops (**Figures 2 and 3**). Drop the thumb loops and tighten all three yarns.

Repeat Steps 2 and 3 for the desired number of stitches; each repeat creates two stitches. Distribute the stitches over your chosen needles and remove the slipknot from the needles (but don't undo it) before joining for working in the round, knitting the "beaded" stitches and purling the yarnovers.

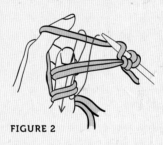

FIGURE 2

Undo the slipknot just before weaving in the tails.

PROS Pretty + very stretchy

CONS Slow to work + takes practice to achieve even tension on the "beads"

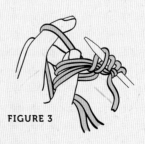

FIGURE 3

Alternating Cast-On

This cast-on looks exactly like 1x1 ribbing at the top of the sock—as though the ribbing just magically begins.

1 Make a slipknot and place it on the right needle; the slipknot counts as a purl and the first stitch. Hold the yarn and leave a tail as for the long-tail cast-on **(Figure 1)**. Work using the two strands coming from the needle; ignore the loops around your thumb and index finger.

2 **KNIT STITCH:** Bring the needle toward you and under the front strand, up between the two strands, then over and behind the back strand to grab it. Pull the back strand under the front strand to make a loop on the needle **(Figure 2)**.

3 **PURL STITCH:** Bring the needle away from you over the strands, then under both the back and front strands. Bring the needle toward you and up to grab the front strand, then pull the front strand under the back strand to make a loop on the needle **(Figure 3)**.

note: When you do this cast-on correctly, the yarn will be looped onto the needle but will not be secured as it is for other cast-ons. If you shake the needle, this cast-on will come undone.

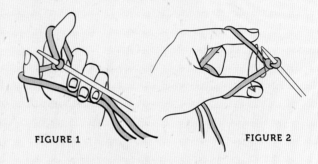

FIGURE 1

FIGURE 2

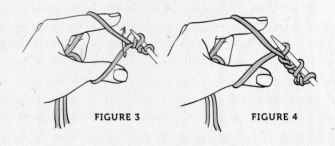

FIGURE 3

FIGURE 4

Repeat Steps 2 and 3 for the desired number of stitches **(Figure 4)**, ending with Step 2 (a knit stitch). Because this cast-on is not "knotted" onto the needle, it's easiest to work one row flat before joining. When turning to start the first row, carry the working yarn to the back around the tail to keep the last stitch on the needle. Work one right-side row flat as follows: *purl 1, knit 1; repeat from * to end. Without turning, join the work in the round at the end of this right-side row.

PROS Stretches as much as the ribbing does + doesn't leave a visible cast-on above the ribbing + very quick to work

CONS Only works for knit 1, purl 1 rib

 TIP

Use a smaller needle if you have one handy; a size 0 is good.

Double-Start Cast-On

This variation of the long-tail cast-on makes a decorative edge.

1 Make a slipknot and place it on the needle. Hold the yarn and leave a tail like you would for the long-tail cast-on method (**Figure 1**). The stitches are made in pairs; the slipknot counts as the first stitch of the pair.

2 **SECOND STITCH OF THE PAIR:** Release the yarn around the thumb, and rewrap it in the opposite direction (**Figure 2**). Bring the needle down through the thumb loop, then under the back strand of the loop (**Figure 3**), then over the strand going to your index finger, then back up through the thumb loop (**Figure 4**). Drop the loop off your thumb and, placing the thumb back in the original V configuration, tighten the resulting stitch on the needle.

3 **FIRST STITCH OF THE PAIR (A REGULAR LONG-TAIL CAST-ON STITCH):** Bring the needle up through the thumb loop then over the strand going to your index finger, then back down through the thumb loop (**Figure 5**). Drop the loop off your thumb and, placing the thumb back in the V configuration, tighten the resulting stitch on the needle.

Repeat Steps 2 and 3 for the desired number of stitches, ending with Step 2. The two stitches worked one after the other result in a strand running in front of two cast-on stitches, which makes them look like a pair. Distribute the stitches over your chosen needles and join for working in the round, beginning your ribbing with a knit stitch.

PROS Can be worked quickly + good stretch

CONS A little trickier than long-tail cast-on

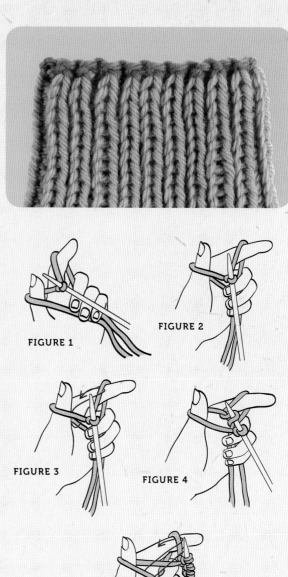

FIGURE 1

FIGURE 2

FIGURE 3

FIGURE 4

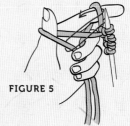

FIGURE 5

Emerging Cable
SOCKS

by **Stefanie Bold**

These cabled socks have an added twist: the gusset decreases are integrated so that the cable panel on the outside of the foot disappears, then emerges from the other side of the heel flap and runs to the toe.

FINISHED SIZE About 6½ (6¾, 7¼)" (16.5 [17, 18.5] cm) foot circumference and 9¼ (9½, 10¼)" (23.5 [24, 26] cm) foot length from back of heel to tip of toe. Foot length is adjustable. Socks shown measure 6¾" (17 cm) foot circumference.

YARN Fingering weight (Super Fine #1). *Shown here:* Spud & Chloë Fine (80% wool, 20% silk; 248 yd [227 m]/65 g): #7804 cricket, 2 skeins. Distributed by Blue Sky Alpacas.

NEEDLES U.S. size 0 (2 mm): set of five double-pointed (dpn), two circular (cir), or one long cir. *Adjust needle size if necessary to obtain the correct gauge.*

NOTIONS Markers (m); st holders; cable needle (cn).

GAUGE 36 sts and 52 rnds = 4" (10 cm) in St st.

notes

* To accommodate different methods of working—double-pointed needles, two circulars, or one long circular—the stitches are divided into two halves, which are referred to as "instep" and "heel" stitches. "Instep" stitches cover the top of the foot and the front of the leg; these stitches are on the first of two double-pointed needles, first of two circular needles, or first half of one long circular needle. "Heel" stitches cover the bottom of the foot, the heel, and the back of the leg; these stitches are on the last two double-pointed needles, the second of two circular needles, or second half of one long circular needle.

* These socks can be worked using a set of double-pointed needles, two circular needles, or one long circular needle for the magic loop method.

Right Sock

CUFF

CO 64 (68, 72) sts. Divide sts over dpn, two cir needles, or one long cir needle (see Notes). Place marker (pm) and join for working in rnds, being careful not to twist sts. The first 30 (32, 34) sts are for front of leg and instep; rem 34 (36, 38) sts are for back of leg and sole.

NEXT RND: K0 (0, 1), p0 (1, 1), work Rnd 7 (4, 1) of Right Cuff chart over 16 sts, [k1, p1] 24 (25, 27) times, k0 (1, 0).

Cont in patt as established, work through Rnd 10, then work Rnds 7–10 four more times, then work Rnd 13 of chart—68 (72, 76) sts: 34 (36, 38) sts each for front and back of leg.

LEG

NEXT RND: K0 (1, 2), work Rnd 1 of Right Cable chart (page 59) over 20 sts, knit to end.

Cont in patt as established for 6 (3, 0) more rnds.

DEC RND 1: Work in patt to end of front sts, k12 (13, 14), ssk, k6, k2tog, k12 (13, 14)—66 (70, 74) sts rem: 34 (36, 38) front sts, 32 (34, 36) back sts.

Work 29 rnds even.

DEC RND 2: Work in patt to end of front sts, k11 (12, 13), ssk, k6, k2tog, k11 (12, 13)—64 (68, 72) sts rem: 34 (36, 38) front sts, 30 (32, 34) back sts.

Work 29 rnds even.

DEC RND 3: Work in patt to end of front sts, k10 (11, 12), ssk, k6, k2tog, k10 (11, 12)—62 (66, 70) sts rem: 34 (36, 38) front sts, 28 (30, 32) back sts.

Work 9 rnds even, ending with chart Rnd 37 (34, 31)–leg measures about 7¾" (19.5 cm) from CO.

HEEL

Heel flap

NEXT RND: Work in patt across 34 (36, 38) front sts and place these sts on a holder—28 (30, 32) back sts rem for heel.

Work back and forth over heel sts as foll:

ROW 1: (RS) K27 (29, 31), k1 through back loop (k1tbl).

ROW 2: (WS) Sl 1 purlwise (pwise) with yarn in front (wyf), purl to end.

ROW 3: Sl 1 knitwise (kwise) with yarn in back (wyb), k26 (28, 30), k1tbl.

ROW 4: Sl 1 pwise wyf, purl to end.

Rep last 2 rows 11 (12, 13) more times, ending with a WS row.

Turn Heel

Work short-rows (see Glossary) as foll:

note: Work wraps tog with wrapped sts when you come to them.

SHORT-ROW 1: (RS) Sl 1 kwise wyb, k21 (22, 24), wrap next st, turn.

SHORT-ROW 2: P16 (16, 18), wrap next st, turn.

SHORT-ROW 3: K17 (17, 19), wrap next st, turn.

SHORT-ROW 4: P18 (18, 20), wrap next st, turn.

SHORT-ROW 5: K19 (19, 21), wrap next st, turn.

SHORT-ROW 6: P20 (20, 22), wrap next st, turn.

SHORT-ROW 7: K21 (21, 23), wrap next st, turn.

SHORT-ROW 8: P22 (22, 24), wrap next st, turn.

SHORT-ROW 9: K23 (23, 25), wrap next st, turn.

SHORT-ROW 10: P24 (24, 26), wrap next st, turn.

SHORT-ROW 11: K25 (25, 27), wrap next st, turn.

SHORT-ROW 12: P26 (26, 28), wrap next st, turn.

Size 6½" (16.5 cm) only

Skip to Shape Gussets.

Sizes 6¾ (7¼)" (17 [18.5] cm) only

SHORT-ROW 13: K27 (29), wrap next st, turn.

SHORT-ROW 14: P28 (30), wrap next st, turn.

SHAPE GUSSETS

SET-UP RND: Sole: K26 (28, 30), pm, k1, pick up and knit 13 (14, 15) sts along edge of heel flap, pick up and knit 1 st between heel flap and instep, k0 (1, 2); Instep: Work Right Cable chart as established over 20 sts, k14 (15, 16), pm, pick up and knit 1 st between instep and heel flap, then pick up and knit 13 (14, 15) sts along other edge of heel flap—90 (96, 102) sts: 42 (46, 50) sole sts, 48 (50, 52) instep sts.

Pm and join for working in rnds.

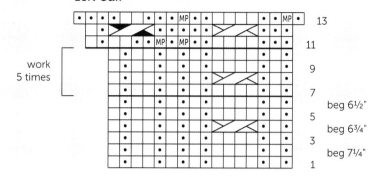

Left Cuff

work 5 times

beg 6½"

beg 6¾"

beg 7¼"

16 sts, inc'd to 20 sts

Right Cuff

work 5 times

beg 6½"

beg 6¾"

beg 7¼"

16 sts, inc'd to 20 sts

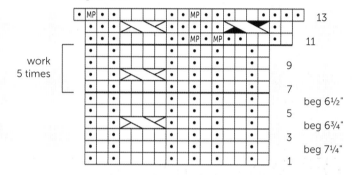

	k

☐ k

• p

╱ k2tog

╲ ssk

⤸ p2tog

⤹ ssp (see Glossary)

MP M1P (see Glossary)

sl 2 sts onto cn, hold in front, k2, k2 from cn

sl 2 sts onto cn, hold in back, k2, k2 from cn

sl 2 sts onto cn, hold in front, p2, k2 from cn

sl 2 sts onto cn, hold in back, k2, p2 from cn

4-to-2 Dec LC: sl 2 sts onto cn, hold in front, [knit 1 st from cn tog with 1 st from left needle] 2 times—2 sts dec'd

4-to-2 Dec RC: sl 2 sts onto cn, hold in back, [knit 1 st from left needle tog with 1 st from cn] 2 times—2 sts dec'd

Left Gusset

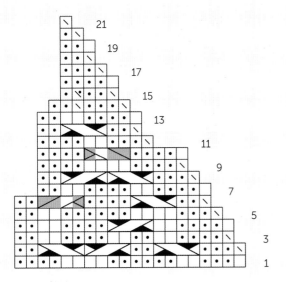

21
19
17
15
13
11
9
7
5
3
1

20 sts, dec'd to 1 st

Right Gusset

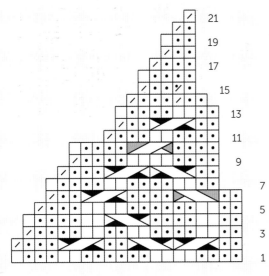

21
19
17
15
13
11
9
7
5
3
1

20 sts, dec'd to 1 st

RND 1: Sole: Knit to m, ssk, knit to end of sole sts; Instep: Work Right Cable chart over 20 sts, knit to m, p2, k2, p1, M1P (see Glossary), p2, M1P, p1, k1, M1L (see Glossary), k1, M1L, p1, M1P, p2, M1P, p1, k0 (1, 2)—95 (101, 107) sts: 41 (45, 49) sole sts, 54 (56, 58) instep sts.

RND 2: Sole: Knit to m, ssk, knit to end; Instep: Work Rnd 1 (38, 35) of Right Cable chart over 20 sts, knit to m, work Rnd 25 of Right Cable chart over 20 sts, k0 (1, 2)—94 (100, 106) sts: 40 (44, 48) sole sts and 54 (56, 58) instep sts.

RND 3: Sole: Knit to end; Instep: Work chart patt as established over 20 sts, knit to m, work chart patt as established over 20 sts, k0 (1, 2).

RND 4: Sole: Knit to m, ssk, knit to end; Instep: Work chart patt as established over 20 sts, knit to m, work chart patt as established over 20 sts, k0 (1, 2)—1 sole st dec'd.

RND 5: Rep Rnd 4—1 sole st dec'd.

Rep last 3 rnds 5 (6, 7) more times, ending with Rnd 19 of Right Cable chart on right side and Rnd 3 (6, 9) of chart on left side—82 (86, 90) sts rem: 28 (30, 32) sole sts, 54 (56, 58) instep sts.

NEXT RND: Sole: Knit to m, remove m, k1; Instep: Work Right Gusset chart over 20 sts, knit to m, work Right Cable chart as established over 20 sts, k0 (1, 2).

Cont in patt as established through Rnd 21 of Right Gusset chart—62 (66, 70) sts rem: 28 (30, 32) sole sts, 34 (36, 38) instep sts. Knit to end of sole.

The new beg of rnd is now after the sole, at the beginning of the instep.

FOOT

NEXT RND: Knit to m, work chart over 20 sts, knit to end.

Rep last rnd until sock measures 8 (8, 8¾)" (20.5 [20.5, 22] cm) from back of heel, or 1¼ (1½, 1½)" (3.2 [3.8, 3.8] cm) shorter than desired length, ending with Rnd 2, 12, 22, or 32 of Right Cable chart.

Cont for your size as foll:

Sizes ending with Rnd 2 or 32 only

NEXT RND: Knit to m, [p2tog] 2 times, 4-to-2 Dec RC, p2, k1, ssk, p2, k2tog, k1, p2, knit to end—56 (60, 64) sts rem: 28 (30, 32) sts each for instep and sole.

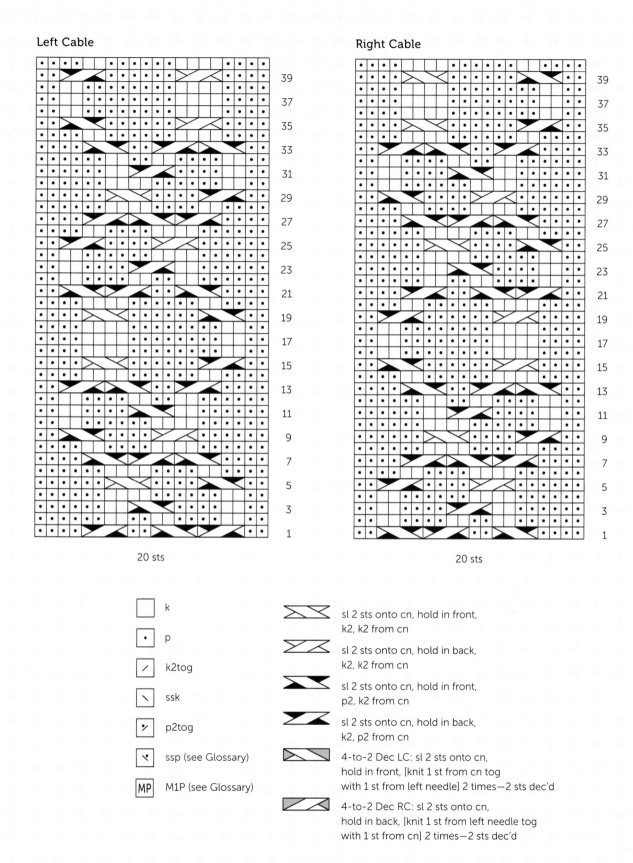

Left Cable

Right Cable

39
37
35
33
31
29
27
25
23
21
19
17
15
13
11
9
7
5
3
1

20 sts

20 sts

	k
•	p
/	k2tog
\	ssk
⟋	p2tog
⟍	ssp (see Glossary)
MP	M1P (see Glossary)

sl 2 sts onto cn, hold in front, k2, k2 from cn

sl 2 sts onto cn, hold in back, k2, k2 from cn

sl 2 sts onto cn, hold in front, p2, k2 from cn

sl 2 sts onto cn, hold in back, k2, p2 from cn

4-to-2 Dec LC: sl 2 sts onto cn, hold in front, [knit 1 st from cn tog with 1 st from left needle] 2 times—2 sts dec'd

4-to-2 Dec RC: sl 2 sts onto cn, hold in back, [knit 1 st from left needle tog with 1 st from cn] 2 times—2 sts dec'd

emerging cable socks

Sizes ending with Rnd 12 or 22 only

NEXT RND: Knit to m, p2, k1, ssk, p2, k2tog, k1, p2, 4-to-2 Dec LC, [p2tog] 2 times, knit to end—56 (60, 64) sts rem: 28 (30, 32) sts each for instep and sole.

All sizes

NEXT RND: Knit to m, [p2, k2] 3 times, p2, knit to end.

Rep last rnd until sock measures 8¼ (8¼, 9)" (21 [21, 23] cm) or 1 (1¼, 1¼)" (2.5 [3.2, 3.2] cm) shorter than desired length, removing m on last round. Pm at beg and end of instep sts.

TOE

RND 1: K1, ssk, work in patt to 3 sts before m, k2tog, k1, sl m, k1, ssk, knit to 3 sts before m, k2tog, k1—4 sts dec'd.

RND 2: Knit the knit sts and purl the purl sts.

Rep last 2 rnds 6 (7, 7) more times—28 (28, 32) sts rem.

Cut yarn, leaving 20" (51 cm) tail.

Finishing

With tail threaded on a tapestry needle, use Kitchener st (see Glossary) to graft rem sts tog. Weave in loose ends.

Left Sock

CUFF

CO 64 (68, 72) sts. Divide sts over dpn, two cir needles, or one long cir needle. Pm and join for working in rnds, being careful not to twist sts. The first 30 (32, 34) sts are for the front of leg and instep; rem 34 (36, 38) sts are for back of leg and sole.

NEXT RND: K0 (1, 0), [p1, k1] 7 (7, 8) times, work Rnd 7 (4, 1) of Left Cuff chart (page 57) over 16 sts, [p1, k1] 17 (18, 20) times, p0 (1, 0).

Cont in patt as established, working through Rnd 10, then working Rnds 7–10 four more times, then working through Rnd 13 of chart—68 (72, 76) sts: 34 (36, 38) sts each for front and back of leg.

LEG

NEXT RND: K14 (15, 16), work Rnd 1 of Left Cable chart (page 59) over 20 sts, knit to end.

Cont in patt as established, working leg shaping, heel flap, and heel turn as for right sock.

SHAPE GUSSETS

SET-UP RND: Sole: K27 (29, 31); Instep: Pick up and knit 13 (14, 15) sts along edge of heel flap, pick up and knit 1 st between heel flap and instep, k14 (15, 16), pm, work Left Cable chart over 20 sts; Sole: K0 (1, 2), pick up and knit 1 st between instep and heel flap, then pick up and knit 13 (14, 15) sts along other edge of heel flap, k1, pm, k27 (29, 31)—90 (96, 102) sts: 42 (46, 50) sole sts, 48 (50, 52) instep sts.

Pm and join for working in rnds.

RND 1: Instep: K0 (1, 2), p1, M1P, p2, M1P, p1, k1, M1L, k1, M1L, p1, M1P, p2, M1P, p1, k2, p2, knit to m, work Left Cable chart over 20 sts; Sole: Knit to 2 sts before m, k2tog, knit to end of rnd—95 (101, 107) sts: 54 (56, 58) instep sts, 41 (45, 49) sole sts.

RND 2: Instep: K0 (1, 2), work Rnd 25 of Left Cable chart over 20 sts, knit to m, work Rnd 1 (38, 35) of Left Cable chart over 20 sts; Sole: Knit to 2 sts before m, k2tog, knit to end of rnd—94 (100, 106) sts: 54 (56, 58) instep sts, 40 (44, 48) sole sts.

RND 3: Instep: K0 (1, 2), work chart patt as established over 20 sts, knit to m, work chart patt as established over 20 sts; Sole: Knit to end.

RND 4: Instep: K0 (1, 2), work chart patt as established over 20 sts, knit to m, work chart patt as established over 20 sts; Sole: Knit to 2 sts before m, k2tog, knit to end of rnd—1 sole st dec'd.

RND 5: Rep Rnd 4—1 sole st dec'd.

Rep last 3 rnds 5 (6, 7) more times, ending with Rnd 3 (6, 9) of Left Cable chart on right side and Rnd 19 of chart on left side and removing all m on last rnd, 82 (86, 90) sts rem: 54 (56, 58) instep sts and 28 (30, 32) sole sts.

NEXT RND: Instep: K0 (1, 2), work Left Cable chart as established over 20 sts, k13 (14, 15), pm, k1, work Left Gusset chart (page 58) over 20 sts; Sole: Knit to end. Cont in patt as established through Rnd 21 of Left Gusset chart—62 (66, 70) sts rem: 34 (36, 38) instep sts, 28 (30, 32) sole sts.

FOOT

NEXT RND: K0 (1, 2), work chart over 20 sts, knit to end.

Rep last rnd until sock measures 8 (8, 8¾)" (20.5 [20.5, 22] cm) from back of heel, or 1¼ (1½, 1½)" (3.2 [3.8, 3.8] cm) shorter than desired length, ending with Rnd 2, 12, 22, or 32 of Left Cable chart.

Cont for your size as foll:

Sizes ending with Rnd 2 or 32 only

NEXT RND: K0 (1, 2), [p2tog] 2 times, 4-to-2 Dec RC, p2, k1, ssk, p2, k2tog, k1, p2; knit to end—56 (60, 64) sts rem: 28 (30, 32) sts each for instep and sole.

Sizes ending with Rnd 12 or 22 only

NEXT RND: K0 (1, 2), p2, k1, ssk, p2, k2tog, k1, p2, 4-to-2 Dec LC, [p2tog] 2 times, knit to end—56 (60, 64) sts rem: 28 (30, 32) sts each for instep and sole.

All sizes

NEXT RND: K0 (1, 2), [p2, k2] 3 times, p2, knit to end.

Complete as for right sock.

Spectrum SOCKS

by **Terry Morris**

Stir some color into your socks with this graphic pattern that's perfect for practicing your stranded-colorwork skills. With a four-stitch repeat, floats of unused color extend no more than three stitches, making it easy to manage tension and achieve a perfect fit. Experiment with colors from across the visible spectrum to make spectacular socks.

FINISHED SIZE About 6½ (7½, 8½)" (16.5 [19, 21.5] cm) foot circumference and 8¾ (9, 10)" (22 [23, 25.5] cm) foot length from back of heel to tip of toe. Foot length is adjustable. Socks shown measure 7½" (19 cm) foot circumference.

YARN Fingering weight (Super Fine #1). *Shown here:* Cascade Yarns Heritage (75% superwash merino, 25% nylon; 437 yd [400 m]/3½ oz [100 g]): #5630 anis (MC), #5610 camel (CC1), and #5618 snow (CC2), 1 skein each.

NEEDLES U.S. sizes 1 (2.25 mm) and 2 (2.75 mm): set of five double-pointed (dpn), two circular (cir), or one long cir for each size. *Adjust needle size if necessary to obtain the correct gauge.*

NOTIONS Marker (m); stitch holder; tapestry needle.

GAUGE 32 sts and 41 rnds = 4" (10 cm) in charted patt on larger needles; 34 sts and 44 rnds = 4" (10 cm) in charted patt on smaller needles.

Cuff

With CC1 and larger needles, CO 133 (154, 168) sts. Place marker (pm) and join for working in rnds, being careful not to twist sts.

RND 1: *K6, pass 2nd, 3rd, 4th, 5th, and 6th sts on right needle over first st, k1, yo; rep from * to end—57 (66, 72) sts rem.

Drop last yo from needle—56 (65, 71) sts rem. Break CC1 and join MC.

NEXT RND: *K2, k1 through back loop (k1tbl); rep from * to last 2 sts, k2.

Change to smaller needles.

Size 6½" (16.5 cm) only

NEXT RND: *K1, p1; rep from * to end.

Size 7½" (19 cm) only

NEXT RND: *K1, p1; rep from * to last 3 sts, k2tog, p1—64 sts rem.

Size 8½" (21.5 cm) only

NEXT RND: *K1, p1; rep from * to last st, k1f&b—72 sts.

All sizes

Cont in k1, p1 rib until piece measures 1¼" (3.2 cm) from CO.

NEXT RND: Inc 4 sts evenly spaced—60 (68, 76) sts.

Leg

Change to larger needles. Work Rows 1–43 of Spectrum chart once. Change to smaller needles. Break CC1 and CC2 and cont with MC only. Knit 2 rnds.

SHAPE ANKLE

DEC RND: K1, k2tog, knit to last 3 sts, ssk, k1—2 sts dec'd.

Knit 3 rnds. Rep last 4 rnds once more—56 (64, 72) sts rem.

Heel

HEEL FLAP

note: The heel flap is worked back and forth in rows centered over the beg of rnd.

NEXT ROW: (RS) K14 (15, 18), turn work.

NEXT ROW: (WS) Sl 1 purlwise (pwise) with yarn in front (wyf), p27 (29, 35), place next 28 (34, 36) sts on holder for instep—28 (30, 36) sts for heel flap.

NEXT ROW: (RS) Sl 1 knitwise (kwise) with yarn in back (wyb), *k1, sl 1 pwise wyb; rep from * to last st, k1.

NEXT ROW: (WS) Sl 1 pwise wyf, purl to end.

Rep last 2 rows 13 (13, 15) more times.

TURN HEEL

Turn heel using short-rows as foll:

SHORT-ROW 1: (RS) Sl 1 pwise wyb, k15 (16, 19), ssk, k1, turn.

SHORT-ROW 2: (WS) Sl 1 pwise wyf, p5, p2tog, p1, turn.

SHORT-ROW 3: Sl 1 pwise wyb, knit to 1 st before gap, ssk (1 st each side of gap), k1, turn.

SHORT-ROW 4: Sl 1 pwise wyf, purl to 1 st before gap, p2tog (1 st each side of gap), p1, turn.

Rep last 2 short-rows 3 (4, 5) more times—18 (18, 22) heel sts rem.

Size 7½" (19 cm) only

Skip to Shape Gussets.

Sizes 6½ (8½)" (16.5 [21.5] cm) only

NEXT SHORT-ROW: (RS) Sl 1 pwise wyb, knit to 1 st before gap, ssk, turn—17 (21) heel sts rem.

NEXT SHORT-ROW: (WS) Sl 1 pwise wyf, purl to 1 st before gap, p2tog, turn—16 (20) heel sts rem.

SHAPE GUSSETS

Rejoin for working in the rnd as foll:

SET-UP RND: K16 (18, 20) heel sts, pick up and knit 15 (15, 17) sts along edge of heel flap, M1 in gap before instep, pm, k28 (34, 36) held instep sts, pm, M1 in gap after instep, pick up and knit 15 (15, 17) sts along edge of heel flap, k8 (9, 10) heel sts, pm for beg of rnd—76 (84, 92) sts.

RND 1: With MC, knit.

Join CC1; do not break MC.

RND 2: With CC1, knit to 3 sts before m, k2tog, k1, sl m, knit to m, k1, ssk, knit to end—2 sts dec'd.

RND 3: With CC1, knit.

RND 4: Pick up MC from under CC1 and with MC, rep Rnd 2.

Rep last 4 rnds 2 more times—64 (72, 80) sts rem.

Break CC1 and cont with MC only. Work Rnds 1 and 2 four times—56 (64, 72) sts rem. Remove all m except beg-of-rnd m.

Foot

Work Rows 1–43 of Spectrum chart once. Break CC1 and CC2. With MC, work in St st until foot measures 7 (7, 7¾)" (18 [18, 19.5] cm) from back of heel, or 1¾ (2, 2¼)" (4.5 [5, 5.5] cm) less than desired finished length.

Toe

SET-UP RND: K14 (16, 18), pm, k28 (32, 36), pm, knit to end.

DEC RND: *Knit to 3 sts before m, k2tog, k1, sl m, k1, ssk; rep from * once more, knit to end—4 sts dec'd.

Rep Dec rnd every 3rd rnd 3 more times, then every other rnd 2 (4, 6) times, then every rnd 3 times—20 sts rem. Knit to m; break yarn, leaving a 12" (30.5 cm) tail.

Spectrum

	MC
	CC1
	CC2
	pattern repeat

4 st repeat

Finishing

With tail threaded on a tapestry needle, use Kitchener st (see Glossary) to graft sts tog. Weave in loose ends. Block lightly.

stranded color knitting
in socks

by **Terry Morris**

Stranded color knitting is the knitter's version of painting by number—and just as simple. It produces intricate patterns using just two different colored yarns per round and a straightforward chart.

But even knitters who have successfully used this technique for other garments may find that their finished socks simply don't stretch enough to fit over their heels. Fortunately, there are tricks to create a more elastic fabric and a successful sock fit.

Even if you get gauge for the stockinette portions of a sock pattern, you may have trouble maintaining it in colorwork areas. Knitters generally find that their gauge is tighter, with more stitches per inch over stranded areas than plain stockinette stitch. A tighter gauge means a tighter sock—one that won't fit. Because stranded colorwork does not have the same stretch capacity as plain stockinette knitting, you have a real problem.

Outside of Sock

Floats Inside Sock

Why Is This Fabric So Tight?

The culprits are the strands, or floats: lengths of yarn not being knitted and simply carried along the back of the work. The knitted loops create the elasticity of knitted fabrics; these straight sections of yarn do not have the same stretch capacity.

Socks fit our legs and feet through the combination of shaping and negative ease. Most socks are knitted a tad smaller in circumference than the actual measurements of your calf and foot; the elasticity of knitted fabric generally allows them to stretch. An inelastic fabric will not "ease," stretch to allow your heel to pass through, or pull in to hug your leg.

What's a knitter to do?

STRETCH

1 Gently stretch out the stitches on your right-hand needle as you strand the unused yarn across the back of these stitches. Aim to space the stitches across the needle more widely than your goal gauge—remember that you will stretch the sock when you put it on. This will ensure that the unused yarn strand will later relax against the back of the work. Avoid over-spacing your stitches on the needle until you've had some success and know how much is too much.

RELAX

2 Let the unused yarn relax on the back side, and be careful not to tug on it when you make the first stitch of the new color. You don't want overly loose, wobbly stitches, so practice until you get it right. Even if some stitches look large when you first try it, you'll be able to wear the socks!

GET BIGGER

3 Try using needles one to two sizes larger than normal for the stranded areas of the sock, especially on the leg portion. Overly loose stranding and a bigger gauge are preferable to short floats and tight knitting. I work the cuff, heel, and toe at about 8½ stitches per inch, then change to a larger needle and work the stranded areas at a gauge of 8 stitches per inch. You can't see much difference between the gauges, but it makes a difference in the elasticity of the fabric.

TURN INSIDE OUT

4 Here's a trick I use for every round of stranded colorwork I knit on my socks: I flip my sock inside out, then knit these rounds. Start by turning your sock inside out on the needles so that you see the right side of the work inside on the needle farthest from you. The wrong side of the sock with the floats will be outside. The outside of the circle has a larger circumference than the inside, which forces you to make your floats a bit longer. The greatest benefit of working this way is you can't inadvertently "jaywalk" your strands diagonally across the corner between needles. This would pull the float tighter than the stitches it should relax against on the back side. With the sock inside out, you can easily see both the color patterning from the previous rounds and the behavior of your floats at the same time.

stranded color knitting in socks

DRIFT AWAY

5 You might have been taught not to let strands go more than four stitches without twisting them in your working yarn, but for socks, let your floats drift across five or six stitches before you consider catching them. Not only is this easier, but your finished sock will look much better. Frequent catching of the floats can make the stitches uneven, cause the fabric to pucker, and reveal dots of the unused yarn color peeking through to the right side. That said, it is important to remember to catch those floats over long stretches of more than six stitches where a color isn't used. You don't want to snarl your toes in the floats when you put on your socks!

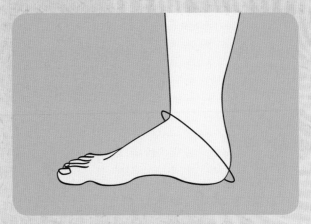

Measure the widest part of your foot (around the instep and heel) and compare with the circumference of your sock in progress.

MEASURE

6 After you've worked a few inches of the stranded colorwork areas on your sock (either on the leg if working cuff-down or on the foot for toe-up socks), it's time to measure. Wrap a tape measure around your foot (or your intended recipient's foot), around your heel and up and over your instep, which is the widest point where the sock will need to stretch the most. Next, measure the circumference of your knitting while stretching it out as much as possible. Compare the two measurements and make sure your sock is able to stretch to match or exceed your foot measurement. You can even try your sock on to do this, taking care not to break your needles.

Measure Your Sock

ADD ON

7 If you find your sock is still too tight, another trick is to add more stitches—especially to the leg portion. Some pattern designers will do this for you. If not, it may be easiest to follow the pattern for the next size up, decreasing the stitch counts for your cuff and heel to fit. If the pattern repeat is a small number, such as the four-stitch repeat in the Spectrum Socks, you can simply increase four stitches after the cuff and work an additional repeat of the pattern. Decrease these four stitches at the ankle before working the heel.

DON'T BE AFRAID TO DUPLICATE

8 Since different colors of yarn are used throughout the patterned areas of the socks (sometimes for only one round!), there are more yarn ends to weave in when finishing a stranded-color sock. To maintain the elasticity of the fabric, use the duplicate-stitch method to weave in your ends on the inside of the sock. The duplicate-stitch weaving closely mimics the path of the yarn in the stitches and will stretch almost the same amount as the original stitches.

BLOCK IT OUT

9 The last step is to block your finished socks with plenty of moisture. Stretch your wetted sock gently in several directions to even out the stitches and floats.

Although these tricks may sound intimidating, stranded colorwork is really fun to knit—and the results are incredibly rewarding.

Duplicate Stitch

✱ TIPS

* ✖ A float should look like a flattened U shape rather than an arrow-straight tight line.

* ✖ If your stitches look inconsistent, don't worry. Over time, most uneven stitches will even themselves out with washing and wearing.

* ✖ If the pattern recommends a U.S. size 1 (2.25 mm) needle, try going up to a U.S. size 1½ (2.5 mm). This odd-sized needle may be a little hard to find, but it is a real treasure in a knitter's tool chest. If your stranded fabric is still too tight, try a U.S. size 2 (2.75 mm) needle.

stranded color knitting in socks

Cataphyll **SOCKS**

by **Hunter Hammersen**

A cataphyll is a specialized leaf whose main job is not photosynthesis. The leaves on this sock trail down the leg then split in two; half continue down the heel while the others wind across the foot. (They do not, however, photosynthesize.)

FINISHED SIZE About 7 (8, 9)" (18 [20.5, 23] cm) foot circumference and 7¾ (8½, 9¼)" (19.5 [21.5, 23.5] cm) foot length from back of heel to tip of toe. Foot length is adjustable. Socks shown measure 8" (20.5 cm) foot circumference.

YARN Fingering weight (#1 Super Fine). *Shown here:* Plucky Knitter Primo Fingering (75% superwash merino, 20% cashmere, 5% nylon; 385 yd [352 m]/3½ oz [100 g]): dandy lion, 1 skein.

NEEDLES U.S. size 1 (2.25 mm): set of five double-pointed (dpn), two circular (cir), or one long cir. *Adjust needle size if necessary to obtain the correct gauge.*

NOTIONS Markers (m); tapestry needle.

GAUGE 32 sts and 48 rnds = 4" (10 cm) in St st.

stitch guide

TWISTED K2TOG
[Sl 1 pwise through back loop (tbl)]
2 times, return 2 sts to left needle,
k2tog—1 st dec'd.

notes

✱ To accommodate different methods of working—double-pointed needles, two circulars, or one long circular—the stitches are divided into two halves, which are referred to as "instep" and "heel" stitches. "Instep" stitches cover the top of the foot and the front of the leg; these stitches are on the first of two double-pointed needles, first of two circular needles, or first half of one long circular needle. "Heel" stitches cover the bottom of the foot, the heel, and the back of the leg; these stitches are on the last two double-pointed needles, the second of two circular needles, or second half of one long circular needle.

✱ This pattern calls for the alternating (tubular) cast-on (page 52). If you prefer, you can substitute any stretchy cast-on.

✱ If you don't have room to repeat Rows 38–43 (49–54, 55–60) of the Foot charts (if you don't have room for the extra leaves before the toe shaping), end with Row 37 (48, 54) of the chart, then skip to Row 44 (55, 61) of the chart, and continue from there.

Right Sock

Using the alternating (tubular) method (see page 52 and Notes), CO 58 (66, 74) sts. Place marker (pm) and join for working in rnds, being careful not to twist sts.

NEXT RND: *P1, k1tbl; rep from * around.

Rep last rnd 5 more times. Work Rows 1–6 of Right Cuff chart (page 74) once—56 (64, 72) sts rem. Rep Rows 1–6 of Right Leg chart (page 74) until piece measures about 5½" (14 cm) from CO, ending with Row 6 of chart.

HEEL FLAP

The heel flap is worked back and forth over last 26 (30, 34) sts of rnd; first 30 (34, 38) sts of rnd will be worked later for instep. Work Rows 1–6 of Right Heel chart (page 74) 4 (5, 6) times.

TURN HEEL

Turn heel using short-rows as foll:

ROW 1: (WS) Sl 1 purlwise (pwise) with yarn in front (wyf), p14 (16, 18), p2tog, p1, turn work.

ROW 2: (RS) Sl 1 pwise with yarn in back (wyb), k5, ssk (1 st each side of gap), k1, turn.

ROW 3: Sl 1 pwise wyf, purl to 1 st before gap, p2tog (1 st each side of gap), p1, turn.

ROW 4: Sl 1 pwise wyb, knit to 1 st before gap, ssk, k1, turn.

Rep last 2 rows 3 (4, 5) more times—16 (18, 20) heel sts rem.

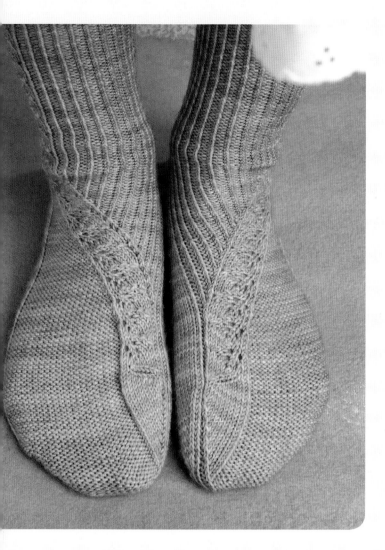

FOOT

Work even through Row 37 (48, 54) of chart. Rep Rows 38–43 (49–54, 55–60) of chart (see Notes) until foot measures about 5¾ (5¾, 6¼)" (14.5 [14.5, 16] cm) from back of heel, or 2 (2¾, 3)" (5 [7, 7.5] cm) less than desired finished length, ending with Row 43 (54, 60) of chart. Work Rows 44–49 (55–61, 61–67) of chart once. Rep Row 50 (62, 68) of chart until foot measures 6½ (6¾, 7¼)" (16.5 [17, 18.5] cm) from back of heel, or 1¼ (1¾, 2)" (3.2 [4.5, 5] cm) less than desired finished length.

TOE

DEC RND: Knit to 3 sts before m, k2tog, k1tbl, p1, ssp (see Glossary), work in patt to 3 sts before m, twisted k2tog (see Stitch Guide), p1, k1tbl, ssk, knit to end—4 sts dec'd.

NEXT RND: Knit to 1 st before m, k1tbl, sl m, work in patt to m, k1tbl, knit to end.

Rep last 2 rnds 4 (6, 8) more times—40 sts rem. Rep dec rnd every rnd 6 times—16 sts rem. Knit to m; break yarn, leaving a 12" (30.5 cm) tail.

Left Sock

Work as for right sock, working Left Cuff, Left Leg, Left Heel, and Left Foot charts in place of Right Cuff, Right Leg, Right Heel, and Right Foot charts, and working toe dec rnd as foll: Knit to 3 sts before m, k2tog, k1tbl, p1, k2tog tbl, work in patt to 3 sts before m, p2tog, p1, k1tbl, ssk, knit to end—4 sts dec'd.

Finishing

With tail threaded on a tapestry needle, use Kitchener st (see Glossary) to graft sts tog. Weave in loose ends. Block lightly.

SHAPE GUSSETS

SET-UP RND: With RS facing, pick up and knit 12 (15, 18) sts along side of heel flap, pm, work Row 1 of Right Foot chart (pages 76–78) for your size over 30 (34, 38) sts, pm, pick up and knit 12 (15, 18) sts along side of heel flap, k8 (9, 10) heel sts, pm for beg of rnd—70 (82, 94) sts total: 40 (48, 56) sts for sole, 30 (34, 38) sts for instep.

DEC RND: Knit to 3 sts before m, k2tog, k1 through back loop (k1tbl), work chart to m, k1tbl, ssk, knit to end—2 sts dec'd.

NEXT RND: Knit to 1 st before m, k1tbl, work chart to m, k1tbl, knit to end.

Rep last 2 rnds 4 (6, 8) more times—60 (68, 76) sts rem: 30 (34, 38) sts each for sole and instep.

Left Cuff

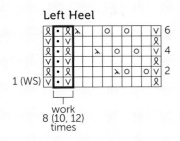

work
8 (10, 12)
times

work
10 (12, 14)
times

Right Cuff

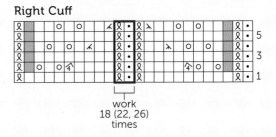

work
18 (22, 26)
times

Left Leg

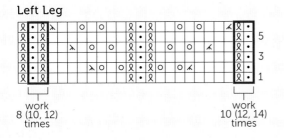

work
8 (10, 12)
times

work
10 (12, 14)
times

Right Leg

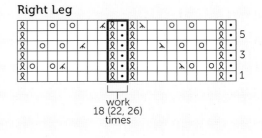

work
18 (22, 26)
times

Left Heel

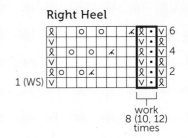

1 (WS)

work
8 (10, 12)
times

Right Heel

1 (WS)

work
8 (10, 12)
times

Left Foot, size 9"

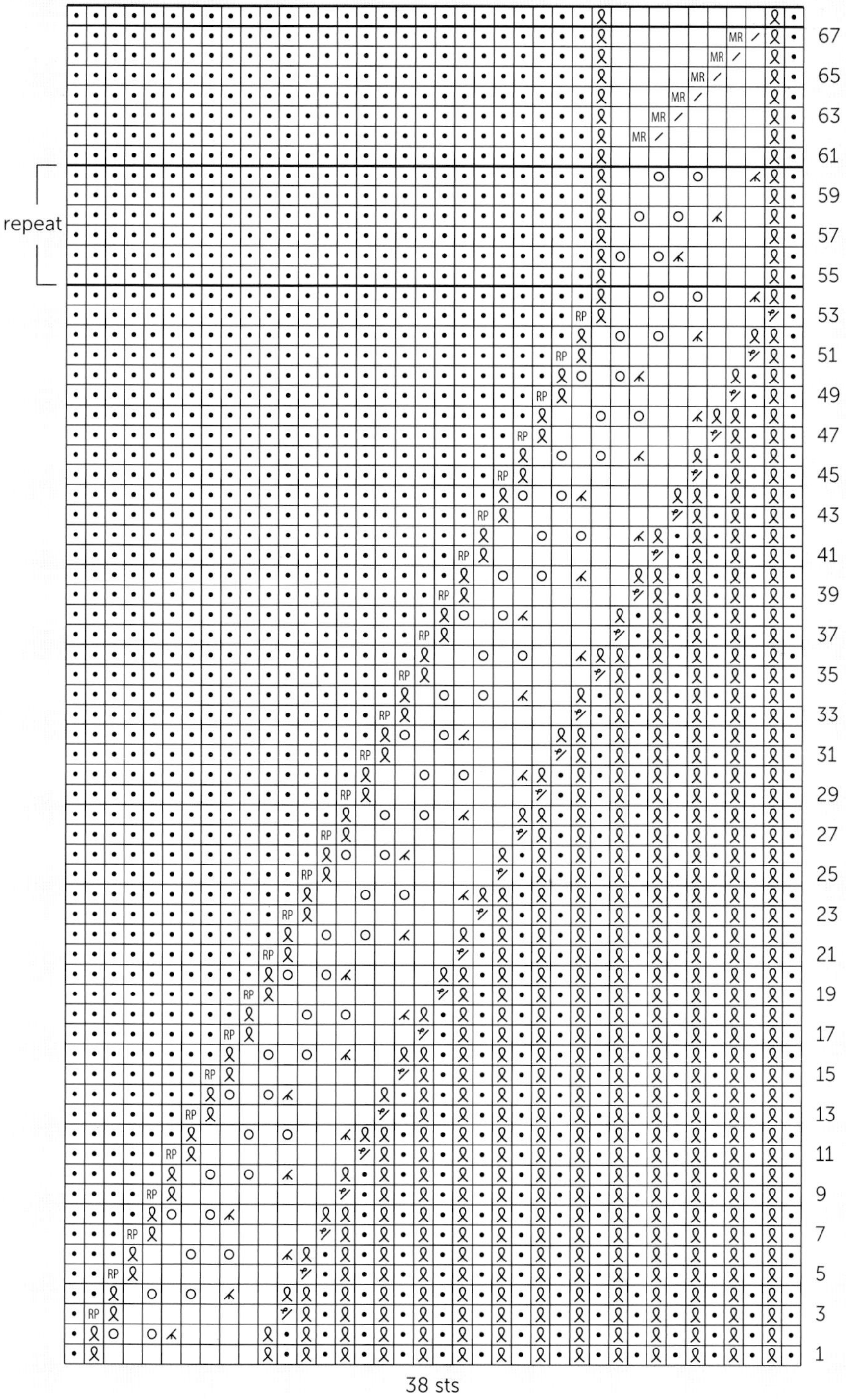

repeat

38 sts

☐	k on RS; p on WS
•	p on RS; k on WS
ℛ	k1tbl on RS; p1tbl on WS
O	yo
╱	k2tog
╲	ssk
⇗	twisted k2tog (see Stitch Guide)
⇖	k2tog tbl
⬈	k3tog
⬊	sssk
⬆	k4tog
⬆	ssssk
V	sl 1 wyb on RS; sl 1 wyf on WS
MR	M1R (see Glossary)
ML	M1L (see Glossary)
RP	M1RP (see Glossary)
LP	M1LP (see Glossary)
�	no stitch
☐	pattern repeat

cataphyll socks

Right Foot, size 9"

Legend:

- ☐ k on RS; p on WS
- • p on RS; k on WS
- ℓ k1tbl on RS; p1tbl on WS
- O yo
- ／ k2tog
- ＼ ssk
- ⟋ twisted k2tog (see Stitch Guide)
- ⟍ k2tog tbl
- ⟋ k3tog
- ⟋ sssk
- ⟋ k4tog
- ⟰ ssssk
- V sl 1 wyb on RS; sl 1 wyf on WS
- MR M1R (see Glossary)
- ML M1L (see Glossary)
- RP M1RP (see Glossary)
- LP M1LP (see Glossary)
- ▨ no stitch
- ☐ pattern repeat

repeat

38 sts

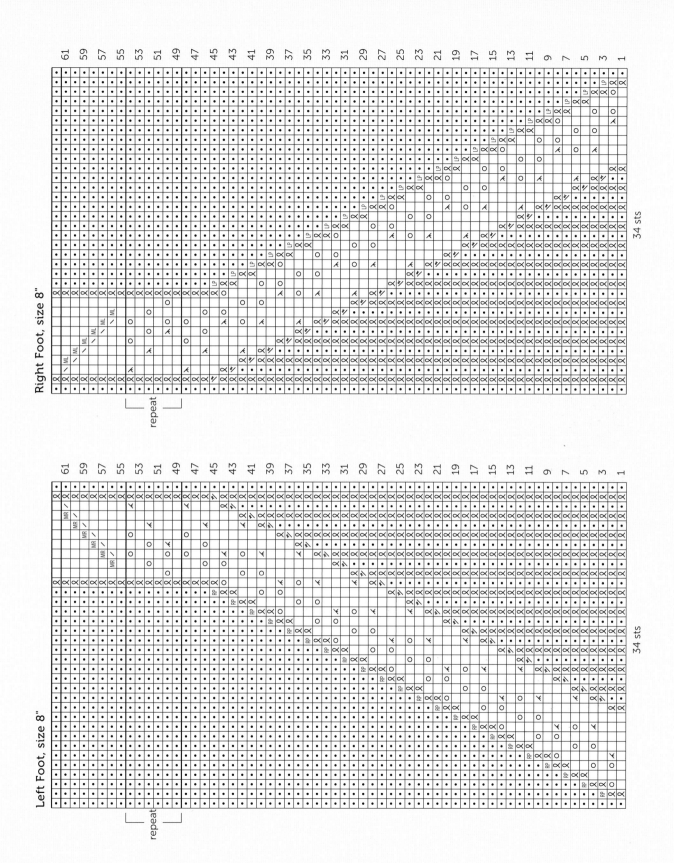

Right Foot, size 8"

Left Foot, size 8"

cataphyll socks

Left Foot, size 7"

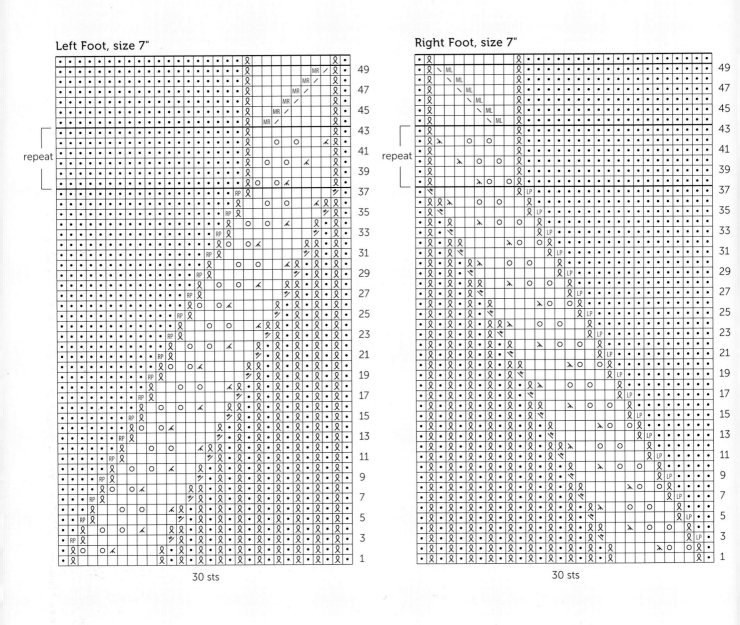

30 sts

Right Foot, size 7"

30 sts

	k on RS; p on WS		k2tog tbl	MR	M1R (see Glossary)
•	p on RS; k on WS		k3tog	ML	M1L (see Glossary)
ℓ	k1tbl on RS; p1tbl on WS		sssk	RP	M1RP (see Glossary)
o	yo		k4tog	LP	M1LP (see Glossary)
/	k2tog		ssssk		no stitch
\	ssk	v	sl 1 wyb on RS; sl 1 wyf on WS		pattern repeat
	twisted k2tog (see Stitch Guide)				

cataphyll socks

Wyeast SOCKS

by **Chrissy Gardiner**

These socks take their name from the Multnomah word for Oregon's Mt. Hood, home of a historic lodge and ski area. The cable patterns, which are reminiscent of ski tracks, were selected by Chrissy Gardiner's husband to ensure they appeal to guys as well as gals. Chrissy opted for cables that are symmetrical top-to-bottom so that they're easily worked either toe-up or top-down if you follow the guidelines on page 84.

FINISHED SIZE About 8 (10)" (20.5 [25.5] cm) foot circumference and 8 (9)" (20.5 [23] cm) foot length from back of heel to tip of toe. Foot length is adjustable. Socks shown measure 8" (20.5 cm) foot circumference.

YARN DK weight (Light #3). *Shown here:* LB Collection Superwash Merino (100% superwash merino; 306 yd [280 m]/100 g): denim, 1 skein.

NEEDLES U.S. size 3 (3.25 mm): set of five double-pointed (dpn), two circular (cir), or one long cir. *Adjust needle size if necessary to obtain the correct gauge.*

NOTIONS Marker (m); tapestry needle.

GAUGE 28 sts and 40 rnds = 4" (10 cm) in St st.

notes

- To accommodate different methods of working—double-pointed needles, two circulars, or one long circular—the stitches are divided into two halves, which are referred to as "instep" and "heel" stitches. "Instep" stitches cover the top of the foot and the front of the leg; these stitches are on the first of two double-pointed needles, first of two circular needles, or first half of one long circular needle. "Heel" stitches cover the bottom of the foot, the heel, and the back of the leg; these stitches are on the last two double-pointed needles, the second of two circular needles, or second half of one long circular needle.

- To facilitate the use of double-pointed, two circular, or one long circular needle, this pattern is written so that the foot stitches are divided into two halves. Instead of referring to numbered needles, the pattern will refer to "instep" and "heel" stitches. "Instep" will refer to the stitches on the first two double-pointed needles, first circular needle or first half of long circular needle and will denote the instep and front-of-leg stitches. "Heel" will refer to the stitches on the last two double-pointed, second circular, or second half of long circular needle and denote the sole, heel, and back-of-leg stitches.

- While the instructions for these socks are top-down, they're a perfect candidate for your first attempt to work a top-down sock from the toe up (see page 84).

Cuff

CO 60 (76) sts and arrange evenly on 4 dpn, circular (cir), or one long cir needle (see Notes)—30 (38) instep sts and 30 (38) heel sts. Place marker (pm) and join for working in rnds, being careful not to twist sts.

RND 1: K1, p2, [k2, p2] 2 (3) times, k1, p1, k4, p1, k1, [p2, k2] 5 (7) times, p4, k4, p4, [k2, p2] 2 (3) times, k1.

Rep last rnd 5 (7) more times.

Leg

NEXT RND: Beg and end as specified for your size, work Instep chart over first 30 (38) sts, then work Heel chart over rem 30 (38) sts.

Cont in patt for 53 (69) more rnds, ending with Rnd 6 of Heel chart and Rnd 6 (10) of Instep chart.

Heel

NEXT RND: Work across instep sts in patt as established (make a note of last chart row worked). Short-row heel will be worked back and forth on 30 (38) heel sts. If using dpns, place all heel sts on a single dpn.

FIRST HALF

SHORT-ROW 1: (RS) K29 (37), wrap next st, turn.

SHORT-ROW 2: (WS) Slip 1 purlwise (pwise) with yarn in front (wyf), p27 (35), wrap next st, turn.

SHORT-ROW 3: Sl 1 pwise with yarn in back (wyb), knit to 1 st before wrapped st, wrap next st, turn.

SHORT-ROW 4: Sl 1, purl to 1 st before wrapped st, wrap next st, turn.

Rep last 2 rows 8 (10) more times. There are 10 (12) wrapped sts on each side of 10 (14) unwrapped center sts.

SECOND HALF

SHORT-ROW 1: (RS) Knit to first wrapped st, knit wrap tog with wrapped st, turn.

SHORT-ROW 2: Sl 1, purl to first wrapped st, purl wrap tog with wrapped st, turn.

SHORT-ROW 3: Sl 1, knit to next wrapped st, knit wrap tog with wrapped st, turn.

Heel

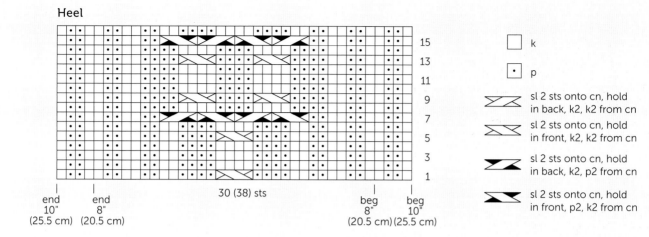

k

p

sl 2 sts onto cn, hold
in back, k2, k2 from cn

sl 2 sts onto cn, hold
in front, k2, k2 from cn

sl 2 sts onto cn, hold
in back, k2, p2 from cn

sl 2 sts onto cn, hold
in front, p2, k2 from cn

Instep

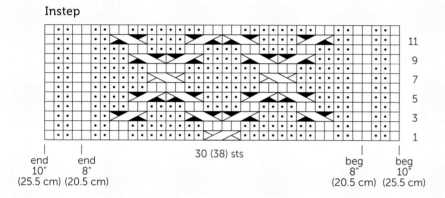

SHORT-ROW 4: Sl 1, purl to next wrapped st, purl wrap tog with wrapped st, turn.

Rep last 2 rows 7 (9) more times—a single wrapped st rem on either side of heel.

NEXT ROW: (RS) Sl 1, knit to last wrapped st, knit wrap and st tog, do not turn.

If using dpns, divide heel sts over 2 dpn with 15 (19) sts on each needle. Resume working in rnds as foll:

NEXT RND: Work instep sts in patt as established, knit wrap tog with wrapped st, knit to end of heel sts.

Foot

Work instep sts in patt as established and heel sts in St st until foot measures 6 (6½)" (15 [16.5] cm) from back of heel or 2 (2½)" (5 [6.5] cm) less than desired finished length, ending with Rnd 2 of instep patt (if needed, end patt earlier and work all sts in St st until foot measures correct length).

Toe

RND 1: Knit.

RND 2: *K1, ssk, knit to last 3 instep sts, k2tog, k1; rep from * once more across heel sts.

Rep last 2 rnds 8 (10) more times—24 (32) sts rem.

Rep Rnd 2 only 2 (3) times—16 (20) sts rem. Break yarn, leaving an 18" (45.5 cm) tail. Divide instep and heel sts evenly between 2 needles and use the Kitchener st (see Glossary) to graft tog.

Finishing

Weave in loose ends. Block lightly.

sock conversions

by Chrissy Gardiner

If you've knitted a few pairs of socks, you've probably discovered your favorite (and least-favorite) construction methods. Here's how to change a pattern to go the way you want it to.

Much of the process of converting a sock's direction of knitting involves reading the pattern in reverse. For example, when working a top-down pattern toe-up, you'd flip to the end of the pattern and start with the toe instructions, then move up to the foot, modify the heel, and finish with the leg, binding off stitches in place of the cast-on directions. A top-down reading of a toe-up pattern would start at the end, too, by casting on in place of the cuff bind-off instructions, then moving up to the leg, working the heel, and finishing with the foot and toe directions.

Which Way Is Up?

Before you work your favorite cast-on and start knitting, you need to determine how the stitch pattern will work in reverse.

A sock with a symmetrical stitch pattern (meaning you can flip it over and it will look the same) doesn't require any tweaking—it can be knitted exactly the same for a top-down sock as for a toe-up sock.

How do you determine whether the stitch you're planning to use is symmetrical? Turn the photo or swatch of it upside down. Does it look the same? If it does, you're all set. If not, you have some decisions to make. Do you like the way it looks

upside down? If so, you can use the stitch instructions as-is. Your sock will look slightly different than the original, but that's not always a bad thing. I designed the Caret + Chevron Socks (see page 18)—which include directions for knitting toe-up and top-down—to look great worked in either direction.

If you don't like the way the design looks when you flip it over (or you really want the sock to look exactly like the original), you'll need to determine whether the stitch pattern can be worked in the opposite direction (see pages 88–89). When I'm faced with this issue, I start by charting out the original stitch pattern. Next, I flip the chart over and try to redraw it going in the direction I need (this sometimes takes a little patience and a lot of experimentation).

Cable stitches (such as the ones in the Wyeast Socks, page 80) are easy to flip. Increases and decreases are trickier because they don't always look the same, so swatch complex patterns to make sure they look good before you start your actual knitting. It's entirely possible that during this process you will invent your very own stitch pattern! Regardless, the goal is to come up with a reversed pattern that you find aesthetically pleasing for your reconfigured socks.

Toes

Once you've got the stitch pattern figured out, the next step is to convert the toe. This is a surprisingly simple process, after working out the stitch pattern and modifying the heel. All you need to do is take the toe instructions from the pattern and work them in an opposite direction.

Consider a top-down sock toe that is decreased on each side every other round for 20 rounds, then closed by grafting the remaining 16 stitches. To convert this to toe-up, you'd start with the 16 grafted stitches. Using your toe-up cast-on method of choice, cast on 16 stitches. Then, increase each side of the toe in place of the decreases, every other round for 20 rounds. Each decrease is replaced by an increase, and when you finish your toe-up toe, you should have the number of stitches needed to work the foot.

Converting a toe-up toe to a top-down one is very similar. Let's say your toe-up pattern tells you to cast on 12 stitches, then increase every other round for 12 rounds until you have 60 total stitches to start the foot. To knit this toe top-down, you'd simply decrease every other round for 12 rounds and then graft the final 12 stitches to close the toe.

A short-row toe is even simpler—work it exactly the same in either direction, but begin the toe-up toe by casting on provisionally instead of grafting (and finish a top-down toe by grafting instead of casting on). A short-row toe is perfectly symmetrical, which is why I chose it for the Caret + Chevron Socks.

If the pattern uses a more complicated toe, such as a star or asymmetrical toe, you'll need to put a bit more thought into the conversion, but the basic idea is the same: Replace increases with decreases when converting toe-up to top-down. Replace decreases with increases when converting top-down to toe-up.

1

The Caret + Chevron Sock, worked toe-up.

2

This is the top-down version of the Caret + Chevron Sock.

Changing Heel Type

Switching a short-row heel for a flap heel, changing the direction of the heel (from toe-up to top-down and vice versa), or even changing both at the same time can be daunting prospects, but it's really quite simple once you have a few techniques under your belt.

Some knitters find that a flap heel is a better fit than the short-row heel. A flap heel is a better choice for someone with a high instep (see page 87), providing extra room for the sock to slip over the widest point of the foot. The extra thickness that's customarily created with a slip-stitch pattern on the flap heel can add a little cushioning and keep the heel from wearing through.

Folks who find the traditional flap heel too baggy or bulbous might just love the sleek cupped shape of the short-row heel. I adore it for complex colorwork patterns because it can be inserted into the sock without any interruption of the pattern (unlike a flap heel's gusset, which can cause all sorts of headaches when it comes to colorwork design). It's also great for self-striping or self-patterning yarns that get thrown off by a gusset and flap heel.

If you want to use every last inch of a precious yarn, you might want to switch from a top-down sock with a flap heel to a toe-up sock with a short-row heel. If you want to make sure the cast-on and heel fit easily over your high instep, you might want to work all your socks from the top down with a flap heel. The best way to determine which type of heel really fits you is to experiment!

If you really like short-row heels, you can place them in any sock you'd like. To work a short-row heel in place of a flap heel, divide the heel stitches (usually—but not always—half the stitches for the cuff) into thirds and work a short-row heel according to your favorite directions. When you've finished working the first half of the short-row heel, you'll have about one-third of the heel stitches wrapped on either side of the remaining one-third of the stitches unwrapped in the center of the heel. Make sure you ignore any gusset increase/decrease instructions when substituting a short-row heel. The heel is worked over the original number of heel/sole/back-of-leg stitches without any net gain or loss of stitches.

Reversing Heel Direction

The short-row heel is perfectly symmetrical and is worked exactly the same in either direction—no changes required! If you're turning a short-row sock pattern over, the heel is the easiest part.

If you have a high instep or simply prefer a flap heel, you can reverse and/or substitute these as well.

When working a flap heel toe-up, you'll need to plan for the heel before you get started knitting so that you know when to begin the gusset increases. (If you're converting a top-down heel flap to toe-up, you may want to start the gusset increases where you see the end of the gusset in the pattern photograph.) Work the gusset along with the instep pattern, then work the heel turn followed by the heel flap instructions. When the heel flap is finished, continue with the pattern's leg as indicated in the pattern.

When working top-down, you'll start the heel flap near the same place you would begin working short-rows—when you've finished the leg of the sock—so you don't need to make any changes before that point. With the instep stitches on hold, work the heel back and forth over the heel stitches. Complete the heel turn, pick up stitches for the gusset, and shape the gusset while continuing to work the instep in pattern.

There's definitely more preparation needed to convert a sock pattern than to knit it as written, but it's a worthwhile investment in your sock knitting (and wearing) happiness to work the pattern the way you like. Besides, while you're making small changes to the pattern direction, maybe you'll try out a different stitch, add your favorite cuff . . . and take the first steps to your own unique sock design.

HOW HIGH IS YOUR INSTEP?

Fitting the instep is a critical part of getting your socks to fit perfectly, but what exactly is a high or low instep? Measure across the top of your foot (in the crease where it hinges to your leg) and around the back of your heel.

The bigger the difference between this measurement and your foot circumference (around the ball of your foot, right next to your toes), the higher your instep. My instep is of average height; it measures 11¾" (30 cm), and my foot circumference measures 8½" (21.5 cm). Thus, the difference between my instep and my foot circumference is 3¼" (8.5 cm). A high instep has a difference of 4" (10 cm) or more, and a low instep has a difference of 3" (7.5 cm) or less. An average instep has a difference between 3" and 4" (7.5 and 10 cm).

sock conversions

FLIPPING STITCH PATTERNS

Here are two examples of charts that need to be converted to work in the opposite direction. The first is a simple V-shaped lace design. You'll see that the lace pattern can pretty much be worked from the original chart turned upside down. Because decreases themselves are not perfectly symmetrical, the pattern is attractive but not identical worked in the opposite direction.

Large V-Lace, Top-down Sock

Large V-Lace, Toe-up Sock

▢	k
•	p
o	yo
╱	k2tog
╲	ssk
⤬	C3B: Sl 2 sts to cn and hold in back, k1, k2 from cn

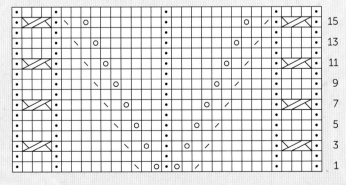

The second example requires a bit more tweaking to ensure that the purl background flows behind the cable ribs appropriately.

As you can see from the charts, the C4F and C4B on Round 1 of the top-down chart need to be switched to a T4F and T4B on Round 8 of the toe-up chart because of what's happening on the next round. The same is true of the T2F/T2B on Round 1 of the top-down chart and C2F/C2B on Round 8 of the toe-up chart.

Heart Cable, Top-down Sock

		knit
	·	purl
		C2F: Sl 1 st to cn and hold in front, k1, k1 from cn
		C2B: Sl 1 st to cn and hold in back, k1, k1 from cn
		T2F: Sl 1 st to cn and hold in front, p1, k1 from cn
		T2B: Sl 1 st to cn and hold in back, k1, p1 from cn
		C4F: Sl 2 sts to cn and hold in front, k2, k2 from cn
		C4B: Sl 2 sts to cn and hold in back, k2, k2 from cn
		T4F: Sl 2 sts to cn and hold in front, p2, k2 from cn
		T4B: Sl 2 sts to cn and hold in back, k2, p2 from cn

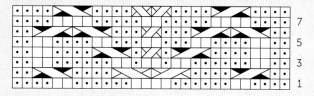

Heart Cable, Toe-up Sock

sock conversions

Uloborus **SOCKS**

by **Claire Ellen**

In search of a spider motif, Claire Ellen derived this subtle, mysterious, and slightly creepy motif from a larger overall floral stitch pattern. Uloborus spiders lack venom and produce a fuzzy type of silk.

FINISHED SIZE About 5½ (6½, 7¼)" (14 [16.5, 18.5] cm) foot circumference and 7 (7½, 8½)" (18 [19, 21.5] cm) foot length from back of heel to tip of toe. Foot length is adjustable. Socks shown measure 7¼" (18.5 cm) foot circumference.

YARN Fingering weight (#1 Super Fine). *Shown here:* Abstract Fiber Mighty Sock (50% merino, 50% Tencel; 382 yd [349 m]/3½ oz [100 g]): little black dress, 1 skein.

NEEDLES U.S. size 1 (2.25 mm): set of five double-pointed (dpn), two circular (cir), or one long cir. *Adjust needle size if necessary to obtain the correct gauge.*

NOTIONS Markers (m); tapestry needle.

GAUGE 36 sts and 48 rnds = 4" (10 cm) in St st.

notes

✖ The leg patterning on the 7¼" (18.5 cm) size sock requires the use of both the Large and Medium Leg charts.

✖ To accommodate different methods of working—double-pointed needles, two circulars, or one long circular—the stitches are divided into two halves, which are referred to as "instep" and "heel" stitches. "Instep" stitches cover the top of the foot and the front of the leg; these stitches are on the first of two double-pointed needles, first of two circular needles, or first half of one long circular needle. "Heel" stitches cover the bottom of the foot, the heel, and the back of the leg; these stitches are on the last two double-pointed needles, the second of two circular needles, or second half of one long circular needle.

Cuff

CO 56 (64, 72) sts. Place marker (pm) and join for working in rnds, being careful not to twist sts.

Size 5½" (14 cm) only

RND 1: *P1, [k1 through back loop (k1tbl)] 2 times, yo, ssk, [k1tbl] 2 times, p2, [k1tbl] 2 times, yo, ssk, [k1tbl] 2 times, yo, ssk, [k1tbl] 2 times, p2, [k1tbl] 2 times, yo, ssk, [k1tbl] 2 times, p1; rep from * once more.

RND 2: *P1, [k1tbl] 2 times, k2tog, yo, [k1tbl] 2 times, p2, [k1tbl] 2 times, k2tog, yo, [k1tbl] 2 times, k2tog, yo, [k1tbl] 2 times, p2, [k1tbl] 2 times, k2tog, yo, [k1tbl] 2 times, p1; rep from * once more.

Sizes 6½ (7¼)" (16.5 [18.5] cm) only

RND 1: *P1, [k1tbl] 2 times, yo, ssk, [k1tbl] 2 times, p1; rep from * to end.

RND 2: *P1, [k1tbl] 2 times, k2tog, yo, [k1tbl] 2 times, p1; rep from * to end.

All sizes

Rep Rnds 1 and 2 until piece measures 1½" (3.8 cm), ending with Rnd 1 of patt.

Leg

SET-UP RND: Work 6 (8, 11) sts in patt, k8 (8, 9), M1 (see Glossary), k8 (8, 9), work 12 (16, 19) sts in patt, k8, M1, k8, work in patt to end—58 (66, 74) sts.

NEXT RND: Work Row 1 of Small (Medium, Large [page 94]) Leg chart over 29 (33, 41) sts (dec'd to 27 [31, 39] sts), then work Row 1 of Small (Medium, Medium) Leg chart to end (see Notes).

Cont in patt through Row 24 of chart, then rep Rows 1–24 until piece measures 5½ (6, 7)" (14 [15, 18] cm) from CO, ending with an even-numbered rnd. Make a note of next chart row to be worked.

Heel

HEEL FLAP

Heel is worked back and forth over first 29 (33, 41) sts; last 29 (33, 33) sts will be worked later for instep.

Work Row 1 of Heel chart (page 94) for your size— 28 (32, 40) heel sts rem. Work Rows 2 and 3 of chart 15 times.

TURN HEEL

Turn heel using short-rows as foll:

SHORT-ROW 1: (WS) Sl 1 purlwise (pwise) with yarn in front (wyf), p16 (18, 22), p2tog, p1, turn work—1 st dec'd.

SHORT-ROW 2: (RS) Sl 1 pwise with yarn in back (wyb), k7, ssk, k1, turn—1 st dec'd.

SHORT-ROW 3: Sl 1 pwise wyf, purl to 1 st before gap, p2tog (1 st each side of gap), p1, turn—1 st dec'd.

SHORT-ROW 4: Sl 1 pwise wyb, knit to 1 st before gap, ssk (1 st each side of gap), k1, turn—1 st dec'd.

Rep last 2 short-rows 3 (4, 6) more times; do not turn at end of last short-row—18 (20, 24) heel sts rem.

SHAPE GUSSETS

Rejoin for working in the rnd as foll: With RS facing, pick up and knit 15 sts along edge of heel flap, pm, beg with chart row noted before heel, work 29 (33, 33) instep sts in patt, pm, pick up and knit 15 sts along edge of heel flap, k9 (10, 12) heel sts—75 (81, 85) sts total: 27 (31, 31) sts for instep, 48 (50, 54) sts for sole; rnds beg at center of sole.

Small Leg

29 sts

Medium Leg

33 sts

	k on RS; p on WS		O	yo		⋏	k3tog		M	M1
	•	p on RS; k on WS		/	k2tog on RS; p2tog on WS		⋀	sl 2 as if to k2tog, k1, p2sso			no stitch
	ℚ	k1tbl on RS; p1tbl on WS		\	ssk		v	sl 1 wyb on RS; sl 1 wyf on WS			

uloborus socks

Large Leg

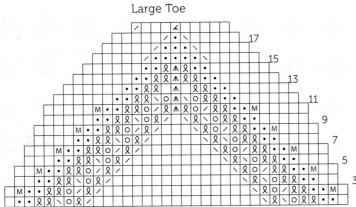

41 sts

Legend

☐	k on RS; p on WS
•	p on RS; k on WS
ℚ	k1tbl on RS; p1tbl on WS
o	yo
/	k2tog on RS; p2tog on WS
\	ssk
⋏	k3tog
⋀	sl 2 as if to k2tog, k1, p2sso
V	sl 1 wyb on RS; sl 1 wyf on WS
M	M1
▨	no stitch

Large Toe

37 sts dec'd to 10 sts

Small Toe

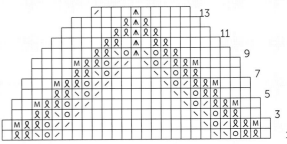

29 sts dec'd to 10 sts

Small Heel

29 sts dec'd to 28 sts

Medium Heel

33 sts dec'd to 32 sts

Medium Toe

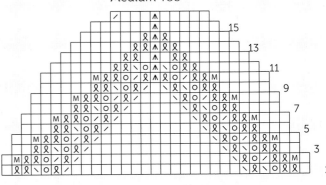

33 sts dec'd to 10 sts

Large Heel

41 sts dec'd to 40 sts

Size 7¼" (18.5 cm) only

NEXT RND: Knit to 5 sts before m, k2tog, k1, pm, k1, p1, remove m, work in patt to m, remove m, p1, k1, pm, k1, ssk, knit to end—85 sts rem: 37 sts for instep, 48 sts for sole.

Work 1 rnd even.

All sizes

NEXT RND: Knit to 3 sts before m, k2tog, k1, sl m, work in patt to m, k1, ssk, knit to end—2 sts dec'd.

Work 1 rnd even.

Rep last 2 rnds 9 (8, 5) more times—55 (63, 71) sts rem: 27 (31, 35) sts for instep, 28 (32, 36) sts for sole.

Foot

Work even until piece measures 6 (6¼, 7)" (15 [16, 18] cm) from back of heel, or 1 (1¼, 1½)" (2.5 [3.2, 3.8] cm) less than desired finished length, ending with an even-numbered rnd—57 (65, 73) sts: 29 (33, 37) sts for instep, 28 (32, 36) sts for sole.

Toe

DEC RND: Knit to 3 sts before m, k2tog, k1, work Toe chart for your size to m, k1, ssk, knit to end—4 sts dec'd.

Work 1 rnd even.

Rep last 2 rnds 3 (4, 4) more times—41 (45, 53) sts rem: 21 (23, 27) sts for instep, 20 (22, 26) sts for sole; Row 8 (10, 10) of chart is complete.

Rep Dec rnd every rnd 4 (5, 7) times—25 sts rem: 13 sts for instep, 12 sts for sole; Row 12 (15, 17) of chart is complete.

NEXT RND: Knit to 3 sts before m, k2tog, k1, work Row 13 (16, 18) of Toe chart for your size to m, k1, ssk, knit to end—20 sts rem: 10 sts each for instep and sole. Knit to m; break yarn, leaving a 12" (30.5 cm) tail.

Finishing

With tail threaded on a tapestry needle, use Kitchener st (see Glossary) to graft sts tog. Weave in loose ends. Block lightly.

uloborus socks

Simply Elegant Cable
SOCKS

by **Judy Alexander**

These socks are an elegant next step in sock knitting—they look complex but require just a few maneuvers. The four-stitch cable is easy enough for a first foray into cables or for mastering the technique of crossing cables without a cable needle.

FINISHED SIZE About 6¼ (7, 7¾)" (16 [18, 19.5] cm) foot circumference, unstretched, and 8½ (9½, 10)" (21.5 [24, 25.5] cm) foot length from back of heel to tip of toe. Foot length is adjustable. Socks shown measure 7" (18 cm) foot circumference.

YARN Fingering weight (#1 Super Fine). *Shown here:* Malabrigo Sock (100% superwash merino; 440 yd [402 m]/3½ oz [100 g]): #37 lettuce, 1 skein.

NEEDLES U.S. size 1 (2.25 mm): set of five double-pointed (dpn). *Adjust needle size if necessary to obtain the correct gauge.*

NOTIONS Marker (m); cable needle (cn); stitch holder; tapestry needle.

GAUGE 34 sts and 48 rnds = 4" (10 cm) in St st.

stitch guide

2/2 LC

Sl 2 sts onto cn and hold in front of work, k2, then k2 from cn.

TWISTED RIB
(multiple of 2 sts)

RND 1: *K1 through back loop (tbl), p1; rep from * to end.

Rep Rnd 1 for patt.

CABLE RIB
(multiple of 11 sts)

RNDS 1–3: *[P1, k1tbl] 2 times, p2, k4, p1; rep from * to end.

RND 4: *[P1, k1tbl] 2 times, p2, 2/2 LC, p1; rep from * to end.

Rep Rnds 1–4 for patt.

notes

✖ The foot will easily stretch an additional inch in circumference.

✖ To help read your knitting and determine when to cross the cable, notice that the last stitch of the crossed cable is a little longer than the other stitches. When you count three regular stitches above the elongated stitch, the next row will be the cable cross row.

✖ To work a left cross without a cable needle (shown below with six stitches), slip the cable stitches one at a time purl-wise to the right needle. Insert the left needle from the front into the crossing stitches on the right needle (Figure 1). Pull the right needle out of the cable stitches. This leaves half of the cable stitches free (Figure 2). Don't panic! Holding the left needle in front of the right needle, insert the right needle into the free stitches, then slip them back onto the left needle.

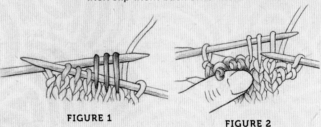

FIGURE 1   FIGURE 2

Cuff

CO 60 (70, 80) sts. Divide sts onto 4 dpn, place marker (pm), and join for working in rnds, being careful not to twist sts. Work in twisted rib (see Stitch Guide) until cuff measures 1¾" (4.5 cm) from CO.

NEXT RND: *M1P (see Glossary), [k1 through back loop (k1tbl), p1] 5 times; rep from * to end—66 (77, 88) sts.

Leg

Work in cable rib patt (see Stitch Guide or chart) until piece measures 8½" (21.5 cm) from CO, or desired length to top of heel, ending with Rnd 4 of patt.

Heel

HEEL FLAP

Center heel on 32 (37, 44) sts as foll: 8 (16, 25) sts from end of previous rnd and 24 (21, 19) sts from beg of next rnd. Place rem 34 (40, 44) sts on holder while heel flap is worked.

Cont for your size as foll:

note: To accommodate a high arch, work additional reps of Rows 2 and 3.

Size 6¼" (16 cm) only

Work 24 sts in patt, turn work.

ROW 1: (WS) K3, [p1tbl, k1] 4 times, p1tbl, k2tog, [p1tbl, k1] 7 times, p1tbl, k3—31 sts rem.

ROW 2: (RS) K3, *k1tbl, p1; rep from * to last 4 sts, k1tbl, k3.

ROW 3: K3, *p1tbl, k1; rep from * to last 4 sts, p1tbl, k3.

Rep Rows 2 and 3 until heel flap measures about 2¼" (5.5 cm) or desired length, ending with a WS row.

Skip to Turn Heel.

Size 7" (18 cm) only

Work 21 sts in patt, turn work.

ROW 1: (WS) K3, [k1, p1tbl] 3 times, k2tog, [p1tbl, k1] 7 times, p1tbl, k2tog, [p1tbl, k1] 3 times, k3—35 sts rem.

ROW 2: (RS) K3, *p1, k1tbl; rep from * to last 4 sts, p1, k3.

ROW 3: K3, *k1, p1tbl; rep from * to last 4 sts, k4.

Rep Rows 2 and 3 until heel flap measures about 2½" (6.5 cm) or desired length, ending with a WS row.

Skip to Turn Heel.

Size 7¾" (19.5 cm) only

Work 19 sts in patt, turn work.

ROW 1: (WS) K3, [k1, p1tbl] 5 times, k2tog, [p1tbl, k1] 4 times, p1tbl, k2tog, p1tbl, k1, p1tbl, k2tog, [p1tbl, k1] 5 times, k3—41 sts rem.

ROW 2: (RS) K3, *p1, k1tbl; rep from * to last 4 sts, p1, k3.

ROW 3: K3, *k1, p1tbl; rep from * to last 4 sts, k4.

Rep Rows 2 and 3 until heel flap measures about 2½" (6.5 cm) or desired length, ending with a WS row.

TURN HEEL

ROW 1: (RS) Sl 1 purlwise (pwise) with yarn in back (wyb), k20 (22, 26), ssk, turn.

ROW 2: (WS) Sl 1 pwise with yarn in front (wyf), p11 (11, 13), p2tog, turn.

ROW 3: Sl 1, k11 (11, 13), ssk, turn.

Rep Rows 2 and 3 seven (nine, eleven) more times, then work Row 2 once more—13 (13, 15) heel sts rem. Knit 6 (6, 7) sts; rnds now beg at center of heel flap.

SHAPE GUSSETS

With RS facing and Needle 1, k2tog, k5 (5, 6), pick up and knit (see Glossary) 1 st in every other st along edge of heel flap; with Needles 2 and 3, work in patt

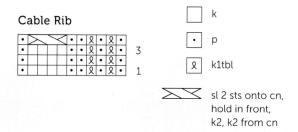

Cable Rib

k

p

k1tbl

sl 2 sts onto cn, hold in front, k2, k2 from cn

across 34 (40, 44) held instep sts (Needles 2 and 3); with Needle 4, pick up and knit 1 st in every other st along other edge of heel flap, k6 (6, 7) heel sts. There should be the same number of sts on Needles 1 and 4.

Working instep sts (Needles 2 and 3) in patt and sole sts (Needles 1 and 4) in St st, work 1 rnd.

NEXT RND: On Needle 1, knit to last 3 sts, k2tog, k1; on Needles 2 and 3, work instep sts in patt as established; on Needle 4, k1, ssk, knit to end—2 sts dec'd.

Work 2 rnds even. Rep last 3 rnds until 64 (72, 80) sts rem; 15 (16, 18) sts each on Needles 1 and 4, 34 (40, 44) sts total on Needles 2 and 3.

Foot

Cont working as established (patt on instep sts and St st on sole sts) until foot measures about 6½ (7½, 7¾)" (16.5 [19, 19.5] cm) from back of heel, or 2 (2, 2¼)" (5 [5, 5.5] cm) less than desired finished length, ending with Rnd 4 of patt. If needed, distribute sts so that there are 16 (18, 20) sts on each needle.

Toe

NEXT RND: (dec rnd) On Needle 1, *knit to last 3 sts, k2tog, k1; on Needle 2, k1, ssk, knit to end; rep from * for Needles 3 and 4—4 sts dec'd.

Work 3 rnds even. [Work dec rnd, work 2 rnds even] 2 times, [work dec rnd, work 1 rnd even] 3 times—40 (48, 56) sts rem.

Rep dec rnd every rnd 8 (10, 12) times—8 sts rem; 2 sts on each needle. Cut yarn, leaving a 12" (30.5 cm) tail.

Finishing

Sl sts from Needle 2 onto Needle 1 and sl sts from Needle 4 onto Needle 3—4 sts on each of 2 needles. With tail threaded on a tapestry needle, use Kitchener st (see Glossary) to graft rem sts tog. Weave in loose ends.

Turnalar SOCKS

by **Leslie Comstock**

Designs in Turkish knitted folk stockings inspired the color pattern of these socks. Leslie's introduction to garter-stitch Jacquard led to the textural contrast between garter- and stockinette-stitch fabrics.

FINISHED SIZE About 5½ (6¼, 6½, 7½, 8¼, 9¼)" (14 [16, 16.5, 19, 21, 23.5] cm) foot circumference and 7½ (8, 8½, 9, 9½, 10)" (19 [20.5, 21.5, 23, 24, 25.5] cm) foot length from back of heel to tip of toe. Foot length is adjustable. Socks shown measure 7½" (19 cm) foot circumference.

YARN Fingering weight (#1 Super Fine). *Shown here:* Cascade Yarns Heritage (75% superwash merino, 25% nylon; 437 yd [400 m]/3½ oz [100 g]): #5606 burgundy (MC) and #5630 anis (blue; CC), 1 skein each.

NEEDLES U.S. size 1 (2.25 mm): set of five double-pointed (dpn), two circular (cir), or one long cir. *Adjust needle size if necessary to obtain the correct gauge.*

NOTIONS Markers (m); stitch holder; tapestry needle.

GAUGE 39 sts and 39 rnds = 4" (10 cm) in leg patt.

notes

✖ To accommodate different methods of working—double-pointed needles, two circulars, or one long circular—the stitches are divided into two halves, which are referred to as "instep" and "heel" stitches. "Instep" stitches cover the top of the foot and the front of the leg; these stitches are on the first of two double-pointed needles, first of two circular needles, or first half of one long circular needle. "Heel" stitches cover the bottom of the foot, the heel, and the back of the leg; these stitches are on the last two double-pointed needles, the second of two circular needles, or second half of one long circular needle.

✖ The two yarns used in this pattern need not both be a solid color; they can be variegated as long as they don't have any colors in common. A variegated yarn is likely to be successful if it gradually transitions from one color to the next, has relatively long runs of color, or if the colors throughout the skein are reasonably close in value (and different in value from the second skein). To get an idea of the values, try looking at the yarn while squinting or taking a black-and-white photo of it. A uniform gray means the values are similar.

✖ When working garter-stitch Jacquard for the cuff, each row of the chart is worked twice. On the first pass the stitches are all knitted following the colors indicated on the chart—just as if working a normal stockinette-stitch stranded pattern. To make a garter-stitch fabric, the stitches on the second pass must be purled. At each color change, the yarn to be used for the next purl stitch must be brought to the front of the work, and to avoid floats across the right side of the fabric, the yarn not being used must be moved to the back before the stitch is purled.

✖ The gusset in this design runs along the center of the sole between the markers. It is worked in alternating one-stitch stripes of main color (MC) and contrast color (CC) bordered by main color. Decreases are worked at the rate of two stitches for every three rounds.

Cuff

With MC and using the Old Norwegian method (see page 50), CO 60 (60, 70, 70, 80, 90) sts. Divide sts evenly over dpn, two cir needles, or one long cir needle. Place marker (pm) and join for working in rnds, being careful not to twist sts.

With MC, purl 1 rnd. Working in garter st Jacquard (see Notes), work Rows 1–16 of Cuff chart (page 105) once. With MC and using the picot method (see Glossary), BO all sts.

Leg

With CC and RS facing, working along WS of cuff about ⅜" (1 cm) from BO edge, pick up and knit 1 st in each CC purl bump (fold BO edge of cuff to RS to see purl bumps)—60 (60, 70, 70, 80, 90) sts. Pm and join for working in rnds.

With CC, knit 1 rnd, inc 0 (0, 0, 2, 0, 0) sts or dec 6 (0, 6, 0, 0, 0) sts evenly spaced—54 (60, 64, 72, 80, 90) sts. Working in St st, work Leg chart (page 105) for your size until piece measures desired length to top of heel, ending with Row 13 (11, 13, 13, 11, 13) of chart, and working rows marked with an asterisk as foll:

RND 3: *With MC, k2 (3, 3, 2, 3, 2), with CC, k1; rep from * to end.

RND 4: *With MC, p2 (3, 3, 2, 3, 2), with CC, p1; rep from * to end.

RND 5: With MC, knit.

RND 6: With MC, purl.

Heel

HEEL FLAP

Break CC; work heel flap with MC only. Place last 27 (31, 33, 37, 41, 45) sts worked onto holder for instep. Heel flap is worked back and forth over rem 27 (29, 31, 35, 39, 45) sts.

ROW 1: (RS) Knit.

ROW 2: (WS) Sl 1 purlwise (pwise) with yarn in front (wyf), purl to last st, sl 1 pwise wyf.

ROW 3: K2, *sl 1 pwise with yarn in back (wyb), k1; rep from * to last st, k1.

Rep last 2 rows 13 (14, 15, 17, 19, 22) more times, then work Row 2 once more.

TURN HEEL

Work short-rows as foll:

SHORT-ROW 1: (RS) K16 (16, 18, 20, 22, 26), ssk, k1, turn work.

SHORT-ROW 2: (WS) Sl 1 pwise wyf, p6 (4, 6, 6, 6, 8), p2tog, p1, turn.

SHORT-ROW 3: Sl 1 pwise wyb, knit to 1 st before gap, ssk (1 st each side of gap), k1, turn.

SHORT-ROW 4: Sl 1 pwise wyf, purl to 1 st before gap, p2tog (1 st each side of gap), p1, turn.

Rep last 2 short-rows 2 (3, 3, 4, 5, 6) more times, then work Short-row 3 once more, ending with 1 gap rem at right edge—18 (18, 20, 22, 24, 28) heel sts rem. Break MC.

ROWS 1–5: Work to m, remove m, work last st of chart, pm for beg of rnd.

ROWS 8–12 (8–12, 8–11, 8–12, 8–12, 8–12): Work to 1 st before m, pm for new beg of rnd (remove old m when you come to it).

NEXT RND: Work 30 (33, 63, 71, 78, 48) sts of chart, pm for new beg of rnd.

ANKLE BAND

RND 1: With MC, knit.

RND 2: With MC, purl.

SHAPE GUSSETS

With RS facing, rejoin MC at end of instep sts.

RND 1: With MC and RS facing, pick up and knit 1 st in corner before heel flap, then 14 (15, 16, 18, 20, 23) sts along edge of heel flap, k1 heel st, k2tog, k15 (15, 17, 19, 21, 25) heel sts, pick up and knit 14 (15, 16, 18, 20, 23) sts along edge of heel flap, then 1 st in corner between heel flap and instep, pm for beg of instep, rejoin CC and work Instep chart (pages 106 and 107) for your size over 27 (31, 33, 37, 41, 45) sts, pm for beg of rnd—74 (80, 86, 96, 106, 120) sts total: 47 (49, 53, 59, 65, 75) heel/gusset sts, 27 (31, 33, 37, 41, 45) instep sts.

RND 2: Beg as indicated for your size, work Row 1 of Right Sole chart (page 107) over 13 (14, 15, 17, 19, 22) sts, pm, [k1 with MC, k1 with CC] 10 (10, 11, 12, 13, 15) times, k1 with MC, pm, ending as indicated for your size, work Row 1 of Left Sole chart (page 107) over 13 (14, 15, 17, 19, 22) sts, sl m, work instep sts in patt.

RND 3: Work Row 2 of Right Sole chart to m, work gusset stripes as established to m, work Row 2 of Left Sole chart to m, work instep to end.

DEC RND: Work Right Sole chart to m, ssk with MC, work stripes as established to 2 sts before m, k2tog with MC, work Left Sole chart to m, work instep to end—2 sts dec'd.

Rep Dec rnd every 3rd rnd 8 (8, 9, 10, 11, 13) more times—56 (62, 66, 74, 82, 92) sts rem: 13 (14, 15, 17, 19, 22) sts each side of gusset, 3 gusset sts, 27 (31, 33, 37, 41, 45) instep sts. Work 2 rnds even.

NEXT RND: Work in patt to m, remove m, with MC, sl 2 as if to k2tog, k1, p2sso, remove m, work in patt to end of rnd—54 (60, 64, 72, 80, 90) sts rem: 27 (29, 31, 35, 39, 45) sole sts, 27 (31, 33, 37, 41, 45) instep sts.

Foot

Cont in patt until foot measures 5½ (5¾, 6¼, 6¼, 6½, 6½)" (14 [14.5, 16, 16, 16.5, 16.5] cm) from back of heel, or 2 (2¼, 2¼, 2¾, 3, 3½)" (5 [5.5, 5.5, 7, 7.5, 9] cm) less than desired finished length.

Toe

RND 1: With CC, knit to m, k1, [ssk] 0 (1, 1, 1, 1, 0) time, knit to 3 sts before m, [k2tog] 0 (1, 1, 1, 1, 0) time, knit to end—54 (58, 62, 70, 78, 90) sts rem: 27 (29, 31, 35, 39, 45) sts each for sole and instep.

RND 2: With MC, knit.

RND 3: With MC, *k1, ssk, knit to 3 sts before m, k2tog, k1; rep from * once more—50 (54, 58, 66, 74, 86) sts rem: 25 (27, 29, 33, 37, 43) sts each for sole and instep.

RND 4: *With MC, k2 (3, 3, 2, 3, 2), with CC, k1; rep from * to last 2 (2, 2, 0, 2, 2) sts, k2 (2, 2, 0, 2, 2).

RND 5: *With MC, k2 (3, 3, 2, 3, 2), with CC, p1; rep from * to last 2 (2, 2, 0, 2, 2) sts, k2 (2, 2, 0, 2, 2).

Cuff

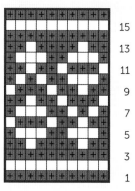

15
13
11
9
7
5
3
1

10 st repeat

Leg, sizes 5½", 7½", and 9¼"

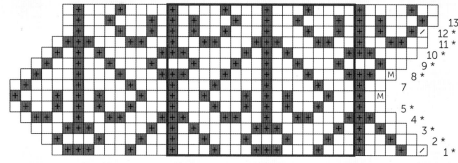

13
12 *
11 *
10 *
9 *
8 *
7
5 *
4 *
3 *
2 *
1 *

* Work as given in directions   18 st repeat

Leg, sizes 6¼" and 8¼"

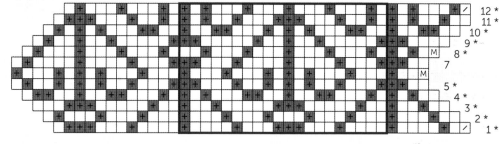

12 *
11 *
10 *
9 *
8 *
7
5 *
4 *
3 *
2 *
1 *

* Work as given in directions   20 st repeat

Leg, size 6½"

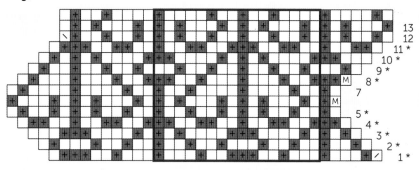

13
12
11 *
10 *
9 *
8 *
7
5 *
4 *
3 *
2 *
1 *

* Work as given in directions   16 st repeat

		MC
		CC
╱		k2tog with CC
╲		ssk with CC
M		M1 with CC
		pattern repeat

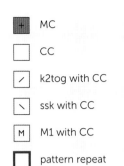

MC

CC

k2tog with CC

ssk with CC

M1 with CC

pattern repeat

Instep, size 5½"

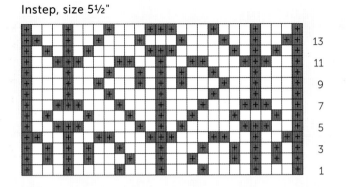

13
11
9
7
5
3
1

Instep, size 6¼"

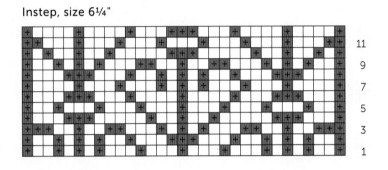

11
9
7
5
3
1

Instep, size 6½"

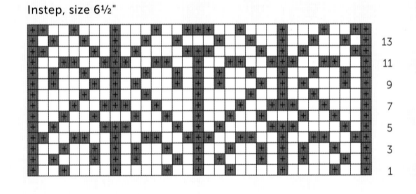

13
11
9
7
5
3
1

Instep, size 7½"

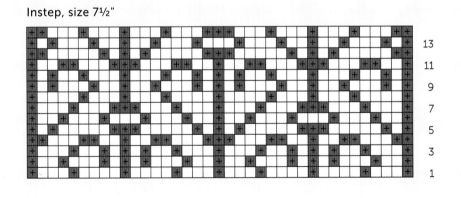

13
11
9
7
5
3
1

Instep, size 8¼"

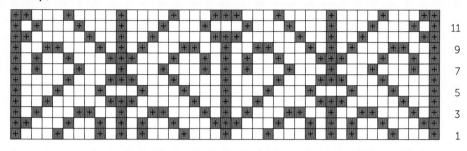

11
9
7
5
3
1

Instep, size 9¼"

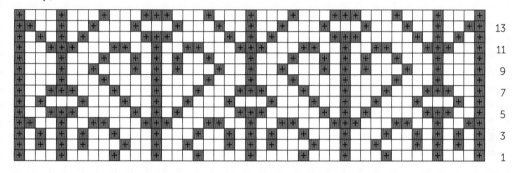

13
11
9
7
5
3
1

Right Sole

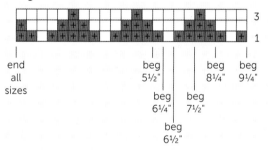

3
1

end
all
sizes

beg
5½"

beg
6¼"

beg
6½"

beg
7½"

beg
8¼"

beg
9¼"

Left Sole

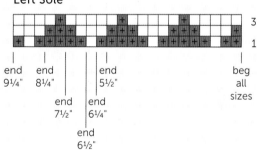

3
1

end
9¼"

end
8¼"

end
7½"

end
6¼"

end
6½"

end
5½"

beg
all
sizes

RND 6: With MC, *k1, ssk, knit to 3 sts before m, k2tog, k1; rep from * once more—46 (50, 54, 62, 70, 82) sts rem: 23 (25, 27, 31, 35, 41) sts each for sole and instep.

RND 7: With MC, knit.

Break MC; cont with CC only.

RND 8: *K1, ssk, knit to 3 sts before m, k2tog, k1; rep from * once more—4 sts dec'd.

RND 9: Knit.

Rep last 2 rnds 4 (4, 5, 6, 7, 9) more times—26 (30, 30, 34, 38, 42) sts rem. Rep Rnd 8 only 3 (4, 4, 5, 6, 7) more times—14 sts rem. Cut yarn, leaving a 12" (30.5 cm) tail for grafting.

Finishing

With tail threaded on a tapestry needle, use the Kitchener st (see Glossary). Weave in loose ends. Block lightly.

Muscadine SOCKS

by **Star Athena**

Start at the toe and knit on up to the top,

then hang a left turn and work the cuff sideways. Slip stitches and unfussy lace pair with garter stitch to create a graphic design reminiscent of grapevines, shown here in a delicious purple color. The cuff is worked mostly in garter stitch, which produces nicely snug and elastic socks. Made in a light sportweight yarn, these squishy socks are quick and fun to knit.

FINISHED SIZE About 8" (20.5 cm) foot circumference, and 10" (25.5 cm) foot length from back of heel to tip of toe; will stretch to 9" (23 cm) foot circumference. Foot length is adjustable.

YARN Sportweight (Fine #2). *Shown here:* Blue Moon Fiber Arts Socks that Rock Mediumweight (100% wool; 380 yd [347 m]/155 g): jasper, 1 skein.

NEEDLES U.S. size 2 (2.75 mm): set of five double-pointed (dpn), two circular (cir), or one long cir. *Adjust needle size if necessary to obtain the correct gauge.*

NOTIONS Markers (m); tapestry needle.

GAUGE 28 sts and 40 rnds = 4" (10 cm) in St st.

notes

✳ To accommodate different methods of working—double-pointed needles, two circulars, or one long circular—the stitches are divided into two halves, which are referred to as "instep" and "heel" stitches. "Instep" stitches cover the top of the foot and the front of the leg; these stitches are on the first of two double-pointed needles, first of two circular needles, or first half of one long circular needle. "Heel" stitches cover the bottom of the foot, the heel, and the back of the leg; these stitches are on the last two double-pointed needles, the second of two circular needles, or second half of one long circular needle.

✳ All slip stitches are worked purlwise with yarn at wrong side of work. On wrong-side (WS) rows, slip stitches with the yarn held to the side of the work facing you.

Toe

Using a toe-up method of your choice (e.g., Turkish, Figure-eight, Provisional, Judy's Magic CO), CO 16 sts. Divide sts evenly among 4 dpns, two cir needles, or one long cir needle—8 instep sts and 8 sole sts. Place marker (pm) and join for working in rnds.

SET-UP RND: K8, pm, k8.

RND 1: [K1f&b (see Glossary), knit to 2 sts before m, k1f&b, k1, sl m] 2 times—4 sts inc'd.

RND 2: Knit.

Rep Rnds 1 and 2 eight more times—52 sts: 26 instep sts, 26 sole sts.

Purl 1 rnd.

Foot

RND 1: [K3, sl 1] twice, k3, k2tog, yo, k5, [sl 1, k3] 2 times, sl m, k26.

RND 2: K4, p3, k6, yo, ssk, k4, p3, k4, sl m, k26.

Rep Rnds 1 and 2 until piece measures 6" (15 cm) from CO, or 3" (7.5 cm) less than desired length from toe to back of heel, ending with Rnd 1.

SHAPE GUSSETS

RND 1: Work instep sts as established to m, sl m, k1, M1R (see Glossary), knit to last st, M1L, k1—2 sole sts inc'd.

RND 2: Work instep sts as established to m, sl m, knit to end.

Rep Rnds 1 and 2 thirteen more times—80 sts: 26 instep sts, 54 sole sts.

NEXT RND: Work instep sts as established to m and place these 26 sts on a holder. The heel will be worked back and forth over rem 54 sts.

TURN HEEL

Work short-rows (see Glossary) to shape heel as foll:

SHORT-ROW 1: (RS) K38, wrap next st, turn work.

SHORT-ROW 2: (WS) P22, wrap next st, turn.

SHORT-ROW 3: Knit to 2 sts before last wrapped st, wrap next st, turn.

SHORT-ROW 4: Purl to 2 sts before last wrapped st, wrap next st, turn.

Rep last 2 rows 3 more times—6 sts rem unwrapped in center of heel; wrapped sts and 15 gusset sts on each side.

Leg

RND 1: *[K3, sl 1] 2 times, k3, k2tog, yo, k5, [sl 1, k3] 2 times; rep from * once more.

RND 2: *K4, p3, k6, yo, ssk, k4, p3, k4; rep from * once more.

Rep Rnds 1 and 2 until piece measures 2½" (6.5 cm) above heel flap or desired length to cuff.

Cuff

SET-UP RND: Work in patt across 13 sts, pm for new beg or rnd.

Purl 1 rnd.

Using the cable method (see Glossary), CO 16 sts onto left needle.

ROW 1: (RS) K11, yo, k2tog, k2, k2tog (1 cuff st tog with 1 leg st), turn work.

ROW 2: Sl 1, k1, sl 1, k1, yo, k2tog, sl 1, k5, sl 1, k3, turn.

Rep Rows 1 and 2 until all but 1 leg st is worked, ending after Row 2.

BO all sts, working k2tog on last 2 sts before BO. Break yarn, leaving a 10" (25.5 cm) tail.

Finishing

Thread yarn tail onto tapestry needle and sew CO and BO edges of cuff tog as invisibly as possible. Weave in loose ends. Block as desired.

NEXT ROW: (RS) K6, [knit wrap tog with wrapped st, k1] 4 times, knit wrap tog with wrapped st and next unwrapped st (3 loops tog), turn—1 st dec'd.

NEXT ROW: Sl 1, p14, [purl wrap tog with wrapped st, p1] 4 times, purl wrap tog with wrapped st and next unwrapped st (3 loops tog), turn—1 st dec'd.

HEEL FLAP

ROW 1: (RS) Sl 1, k1, [sl 1, k3] 2 times, k2tog, yo, k5, sl 1, k3, sl 1, k1, ssk (1 heel st tog with 1 gusset st), turn—1 st dec'd.

ROW 2: Sl 1, p2, k3, p4, ssp (see Glossary), yo, p6, k3, p2, p2tog (1 heel st tog with 1 gusset st), turn.

Rep last 2 rows 11 more times—2 gusset sts rem on each side.

NEXT ROW: (RS) Sl 1, k1, [sl 1, k3] 2 times, k2tog, yo, k5, sl 1, k3, sl 1, k1, ssk, k1, do not turn.

Resume working in rnds as foll:

NEXT RND: Pm for beg of instep, [k3, sl 1] 2 times, k3, k2tog, yo, k5, [sl 1, k3] 2 times, pm for new beg-of-rnd, k1, k2tog, k2, p3, k6, yo, ssk, k4, p3, k4, sl m, k4, p3, k6, yo, ssk, k4, p3, k4—52 sts rem.

bind-offs **for toe-up socks**

by **Karen Frisa**

The perfect toe-up socks can be ruined by a too-tight bind-off. For a beautiful (and beautifully fitting) cuff, try one of these favorites.

Doubled Bind-Off

Also called a decrease bind-off, this method is related to the standard bind-off, but it has more give.

YOU WILL NEED Your knitting needles and enough working yarn to knit about 2 rounds, plus a tapestry needle for weaving in ends.

1 K1, *k1, insert left needle into fronts of 2 stitches on right needle **(Figure 1)** and knit them tog through back loop (tbl); rep from * around.

2 To make a seamless join at the end of the bind-off, cut the yarn, leaving a 6" (15 cm) tail. Pull the last stitch on the right needle, making it bigger, until the tail pops through and the last stitch disappears. Thread the tail onto a tapestry needle. Insert the tapestry needle under the legs of the first stitch of the bind-off, which looks like the start of a crocheted chain, and pull the yarn through. Then insert the tapestry needle into the top of the last stitch bound off (the same place where the tail comes out) and snug until the new chain blends with the other bind-off chains **(Figure 2)**. Weave in ends. This produces a continuous chain around the bound-off edge.

PROS No grafting or sewing required

CONS Not as elastic as other methods

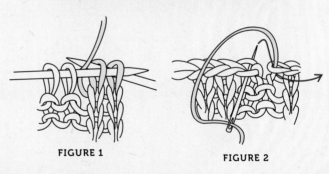

FIGURE 1   FIGURE 2

 TIP

Using a larger needle in your right hand will make this bind-off loose.

Invisible Sewn Bind-Off

This bind-off makes an unassuming, attractive edge that is surprisingly elastic. It's especially effective for a garter-stitch cuff, but it also works well for ribbing.

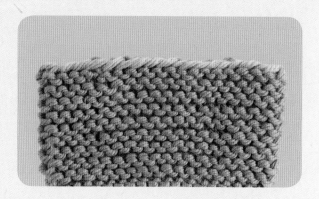

YOU WILL NEED A tapestry needle and a yarn tail 4 times the circumference of your sock.

1 Thread the tail onto a tapestry needle.

2 Insert the tapestry needle knitwise (kwise) into the second stitch on the left needle and pull the yarn through to the back. Insert the tapestry needle purlwise (pwise) into the first stitch on the left needle (**Figure 1**), pull the yarn through to the front, and transfer this stitch pwise to the right needle. Repeat this step once more.

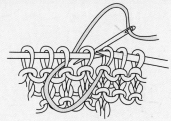

FIGURE 1

3 Insert the tapestry needle kwise into the second stitch on the left needle and pull the yarn through. Insert the tapestry needle pwise into the first stitch on the left needle (**Figure 2**) and pull the yarn through (**Figure 3**; blue yarn). Drop the first stitch off the left needle. Repeat this step until 2 stitches remain.

FIGURE 2

4 Insert the tapestry needle kwise into the second stitch on the left needle (**Figure 3**; red arrow) and pull the yarn through. Drop both stitches off the left needle.

PROS Very stretchy and unobtrusive; works for a variety of stitch patterns

CONS Can be a bit fiddly to work

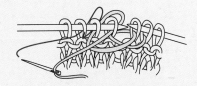

FIGURE 3

VARIATION

To make the purl bumps show on the right side of the work, substitute "pwise" for "kwise" and "kwise" for "pwise" in the above instructions.

 TIP

Don't pull the working yarn too tightly; make sure there is enough give for the bind-off edge to remain stretchy.

Kitchener Bind-Off

This makes a beautiful edge for 1×1 rib (or 2×2 rib; see variation). It works like a standard Kitchener stitch, dividing the stitches onto two needles and grafting them together.

YOU WILL NEED Two spare double-pointed or circular needles (can be smaller than the ones used for your sock); a tapestry needle; and a yarn tail 4 times the circumference of your sock.

1 Arrange stitches so that the first stitch on the left needle is a knit stitch. If your first stitch is a purl, purl it onto the right needle so that the first stitch on the left needle is a knit.

2 Using the two spare needles, slip the knit stitches onto one needle and the purl stitches onto another. (Slip about one-third to one-fourth of your total stitches to begin; as you work the stitches off, you can transfer more.) Hold the needle with the knit stitches to the front and the needle with the purl stitches behind it.

3 With the tail threaded on a tapestry needle, insert the tapestry needle knitwise (kwise) into the first stitch on the front needle, transfer this stitch to the right needle, then insert the tapestry needle purlwise (pwise) into the next stitch on the front needle and pull the yarn through **(Figure 1)**.

4 Insert the tapestry needle pwise into the first stitch on the back needle, transfer this stitch to the right needle, then insert the tapestry needle kwise into the next stitch on the back needle and pull the yarn through **(Figure 2)**.

5 Insert the tapestry needle kwise into the first stitch on the front needle and slip it onto the tapestry needle, then insert the tapestry needle pwise into the next stitch on the front needle and pull the yarn through; don't drop this stitch off the front needle.

6 Insert the tapestry needle pwise into the first stitch on the back needle and slip it onto the tapestry needle, then insert the tapestry needle kwise into the next stitch on the back needle and

pull the yarn through; don't drop this stitch off the back needle.

Repeat Steps 3–6 until one stitch remains on each needle. Drop these stitches off the needles.

PROS Invisible and very stretchy

CONS Only works for 1×1 and 2×2 ribbing; requires grafting

VARIATION

For 2×2 rib, begin with a single knit stitch on the left needle (followed by two purl stitches). If the left needle begins with two knit stitches, knit the first stitch onto the right needle. Proceed as for 1×1 rib.

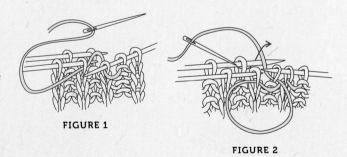

FIGURE 1

FIGURE 2

 TIP

After every few stitches, pull on the bound-off edge to make sure it has enough give. Don't pull the bind-off too tight.

Sideways Bind-Off

This isn't really a bind-off at all; it's a way to secure the stitches on the needle while adding a decorative edge. It's just like working a sideways edging on a shawl.

Because there isn't really a bound-off edge, you don't have to worry about having enough stretch in the bind-off. General instructions are given here, but any stitch pattern can be used.

YOU WILL NEED A spare double-pointed or straight needle in the same size as for the rest of the sock, plenty of working yarn, and a tapestry needle to weave in ends.

1 Cast on the number of stitches needed for your edging.

2 (RS) Work in cuff patt to last edging st, ssk (last edging st tog with next sock st), turn work.

3 (WS) Work in patt to end of edging and just the edging stitches remain.

4 Repeat Steps 2 and 3 **(Figure 1)** until all sock stitches have been joined to the edging.

5 Sew the remaining live stitches to the cast-on stitches.

PROS This is an opportunity to add a stitch pattern, such as lace or a cabled edging, to complement the rest of the sock. (See the Muscadine Socks on page 108 for one example.)

CONS Requires more yarn than other bind-offs

VARIATION

Begin with the provisional cast-on of your choice. After working all the way around the sock, remove the provisional cast-on and graft the revealed stitches to the live edging stitches.

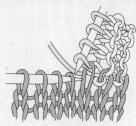

FIGURE 1

✳ **TIP**

Replacing the ssk with a different decrease gives a different effect. Try k2tog, k2tog tbl, p2tog, ssp, etc.

Frost Feather STOCKINGS

by Deborah Newton

Imagining an old-fashioned "wedding stocking," Deborah Newton created these lacy yet rustic over-the-knee socks. Beginning with a wide rib, an array of lace patterns gradually decreases in width to shape the stocking. As intricate as the ice crystals on a wintry windowpane, these lovely stockings will keep you warm on the coldest day.

FINISHED SIZE *Foot:* About 7½ (8)" (19 [20.5] cm) circumference; foot length is adjustable. *Ankle:* 7 (7½)" (18 [19] cm) circumference above heel flap, slightly stretched. *Calf:* 12" (30.5 cm) unstretched; 16" (40.5 cm) stretched. Socks shown measure 7½" (19 cm) foot circumference.

YARN Sportweight (Fine #2). *Shown here:* Quince & Co. Chickadee (100% wool; 181 yd [166 m]/50 g): #105 glacier, 5 skeins.

NEEDLES U.S. size 3 (3.25 mm): set of five double-pointed (dpn). *Adjust needle size if necessary to obtain the correct gauge.*

NOTIONS Marker (m); tapestry needle; 1¾ yd (1.6 m) of ½" (1.3 cm) wide stiff ribbon (optional).

GAUGE 26 sts and 36 rnds = 4" (10 cm) in St st; 25 sts = 4" (10 cm) in Chevron patt.

stitch guide

RIGHT TWIST (RT; WORKED OVER 2 STS)

Knit second st on left needle and leave on left needle, then knit first st on left needle. Drop both sts from left needle.

notes

- Upper leg portion of socks is designed in one size. To adjust the size of the leg, consider altering your gauge slightly by using larger or smaller needles.

Cuff

CO 99 sts. Divide sts as evenly as possible over 4 dpn, place marker (pm), and join for working in the rnd, being careful not to twist sts.

Work Top Rib chart (page 120) for 4" (10 cm).

NEXT RND: [K18, k2tog] 4 times, k17, k2tog—94 sts rem.

Leg

CHEVRON SECTION

Rearrange sts as foll: 25 sts each on Needles 1 and 3, 22 sts each on Needles 2 and 4.

NEXT RND: *On Needle 1, work Chevron chart (page 120); on Needle 2, work Textured Rib chart (page 120); rep from * on Needles 3 and 4.

Work even in patt for 46 more rnds, ending with Row 15 of Chevron chart and Row 3 of Textured Rib chart.

NEXT RND: *On Needle 1, k8, ssk, k5, k2tog, knit to end; on Needle 2, work in patt as established; rep from * for Needles 3 and 4—90 sts rem: 23 sts each on Needles 1 and 3, 22 sts each on Needles 2 and 4.

SMALL CHEVRON SECTION

NEXT RND: *On Needle 1, work Small Chevron chart (page 120); on Needle 2, work in patt as established; rep from * for Needles 3 and 4.

Cont in patt for 11 more rnds, ending with Row 12 of Small Chevron chart and Row 4 of Textured Rib chart.

NEXT RND: *On Needle 1, work Row 13 of Small Chevron chart; on Needle 2, work Mock Cable chart (page 120); rep from * for Needles 3 and 4.

Cont in patt for 16 more rnds, ending with Row 9 of Small Chevron chart and Row 1 of Mock Cable chart.

NEXT RND: (dec rnd) *On Needle 1, k2, ssk, p1, p2tog, k1, sl 2 as if to k2tog, k1, p2sso, k1, sl 2 as if to k2tog, k1, p2sso, k1, p2tog, p1, k2tog, k2; on Needle 2, work in patt as established; rep from * for Needles 3 and 4—74 sts rem: 15 sts each on Needles 1 and 3, 22 sts each on Needles 2 and 4.

LEAF SECTION

note: *Stitch count changes from rnd to rnd for this patt; count sts after Rows 1–4, 11, and 12 of Leaf chart.*

NEXT RND: *On Needle 1, work Leaf chart (page 120); on Needle 2, work in patt as established; rep from * for Needles 3 and 4.

Cont in patt for 35 more rnds, ending with Row 12 of Leaf chart and Row 2 of Mock Cable chart.

NEXT RND: (dec rnd) *On Needle 1, work Row 1 of Leaf chart; on Needle 2, p2, [k2tog] 3 times, p2, k2, p2, [k2tog] 3 times, p2; rep from * for Needles 3 and 4—62 sts rem: 15 sts each on Needles 1 and 3, 16 sts each on Needles 2 and 4.

NEXT RND: *On Needle 1, work Row 2 of Leaf chart; on Needle 2, work Row 1 of Eyelet Rib chart (page 120); rep from * for Needles 3 and 4.

Cont in patt for 21 more rnds, ending with Row 11 of Leaf chart and Row 2 of Eyelet Rib chart—piece measures about 15" (38 cm) below ribbing.

DIAMOND SECTION

NEXT RND: (dec rnd) *On Needle 1, k1, [k2tog] 2 (1) time(s), k5 (9), [ssk] 2 (1) time(s), k1; on Needle 2, cont in patt as established; rep from * for Needles 3 and 4—54 (58) sts rem: 11 (13) sts each on Needles 1 and 3, 16 sts each on Needles 2 and 4.

NEXT RND: *On Needle 1, knit; on Needle 2, cont in patt as established; rep from * for Needles 3 and 4.

NEXT RND: *On Needle 1, work 2 (3) sts in St st, work Diamond chart (page 120), work 2 (3) sts in St st; on Needle 2, cont in patt as established; rep from * for Needles 3 and 4.

Cont in patt for 19 more rnds, ending with Row 10 of Diamond chart and Row 4 of Eyelet Rib chart.

Size 7½" (19 cm) only

NEXT RND: (dec rnd) *On Needle 1, k2tog, work next row of Diamond chart, k2tog; on Needle 2, work 7 sts in patt, k2tog in center k2 rib (keep resulting st in St st), work 7 sts in patt; rep from * for Needles 3 and 4—48 sts rem: 9 sts each on Needles 1 and 3, 15 sts each on Needles 2 and 4.

Both sizes

Cont in patt for 19 (20) more rnds, ending with Row 10 of Diamond chart and Row 4 of Eyelet Rib chart—piece measures about 20" (51 cm) below ribbing.

Ankle

Size 7½" (19 cm) only

NEXT RND: Knit 1 rnd, inc 1 st on Needle 2 and dec 1 st on Needle 4—48 sts total: 9 sts each on Needles 1 and 3, 16 sts each on Needle 2, 14 sts on Needle 4. Break yarn.

Skip to Heel.

Size 8" (20 cm) only

NEXT RND: Knit 1 rnd, dec 3 sts on Needles 1 and 3—52 sts total: 10 sts each on Needles 1 and 3, 16 sts each on Needles 2 and 4. Break yarn.

Heel

Rearrange sts onto 3 dpn as foll: sl 4 (5) sts each from Needles 1 and 3 onto Needle 2 for heel. Note that this aligns the lace panels at sides of leg. Divide rem 24 (26) sts evenly on the other 2 dpn to work later for instep—12 (13) sts each on Needles 1 and 3, 24 (26) sts on Needle 2.

HEEL FLAP

With RS facing, join yarn to beg of sts on heel needle.

ROW 1: (RS) *Sl 1 purlwise (pwise) with yarn in back (wyb), k1; rep from * to end.

ROW 2: (WS) Sl 1 pwise with yarn in front (wyf), purl to end.

frost feather stockings

Top Rib

9-st repeat

Textured Rib

Eyelet Rib

	k			k3tog
•	p	⊀		sl 1, k2tog, psso
ↄ	k1tbl			k3tog tbl
O	yo	↑		sl 2 as if to k2tog, k1, p2sso
╱	k2tog	☐		pattern repeat
╲	ssk			right twist (see Stitch Guide)

Chevron

Diamond

Mock Cable

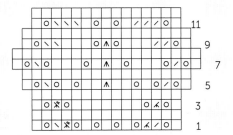

Small Chevron

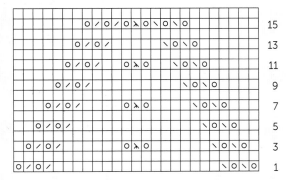

Leaf

Rep Rows 1 and 2 eleven (twelve) more times, then work Row 1 once more—25 (27) heel flap rows; heel flap measures about 2 (2¼)" (5 [5.5] cm).

TURN HEEL

Shape heel using short-rows as foll:

ROW 1: (WS) P14 (15), p2tog, p1, turn work.

ROW 2: (RS) Sl 1 pwise wyb, k5, ssk, k1, turn.

ROW 3: Sl 1 pwise wyf, purl to 1 st before gap formed by previous row, p2tog (1 st each side of gap), p1, turn—1 st dec'd.

ROW 4: Sl 1 pwise wyb, knit to 1 st before gap formed by previous row, ssk (1 st each side of gap), k1, turn—1 st dec'd.

Rep Rows 3 and 4 three more times, ending with a RS row and omitting k1 or p1 after dec on last rep for smaller size—14 (16) heel sts rem. Break yarn.

SHAPE GUSSETS

Divide heel sts evenly onto 2 dpn; rnds beg at center of heel.

RND 1: With Needle 1 and RS facing, rejoin yarn and k7 (8) heel sts, pick up and knit (see Glossary) 12 (13) sts along left edge of heel flap; with Needle 2, k24 (26) instep sts; with Needle 3, pick up and knit 12 (13) sts along right edge of heel flap, k7 (8) heel sts—62 (68) sts total: 19 (21) sts each on Needles 1 and 3, 24 (26) sts on Needle 2.

RND 2: Knit.

RND 3: (dec rnd) On Needle 1, knit to last 3 sts, k2tog, k1; on Needle 2, k24 (26); on Needle 3, k1, ssk, knit to end—2 sts dec'd.

RND 4: Knit.

Rep Rnds 3 and 4 six (seven) more times—48 (52) sts rem: 12 (13) sts each on Needles 1 and 3, 24 (26) sts on Needle 2.

Foot

Work even in St st for 7 (5) more rnds.

NEXT RND: On Needle 1, knit; on Needle 2, k8 (10), work Row 1 of Diamond chart, k9; on Needle 3, knit.

Work even in patt for 19 more rnds, ending with Row 10 of chart.

Work even in St st until foot measures 7¼ (7¾)" (18.5 [19.5] cm) from back of heel, or 2" (5 cm) less than desired finished length.

NEXT RND: (eyelet rnd) On Needles 1 and 3, knit; on Needle 2, k1, *k2tog, yo; rep from * to last st, k1.

Work even until foot measures 7½ (8)" (19 [20.5] cm), or desired length from back of heel.

Toe

RND 1: (dec rnd) On Needle 1, knit to last 3 sts, k2tog, k1; on Needle 2, k1, ssk, knit to last 3 sts, k2tog, k1; on Needle 3, k1, ssk, knit to end—4 sts dec'd.

RND 2: Knit.

Rep Rnds 1 and 2 five (six) more times—24 sts rem. K6 from Needle 1 onto Needle 3. Cut yarn, leaving a 12" (30.5 cm) tail.

Finishing

With tail threaded on a tapestry needle, use Kitchener st (see Glossary) to graft rem sts tog. Weave in loose ends. Steam sock lightly; do not flatten or press rib. Cut ribbon in half. Thread each half through eyelets in top rib, about 2" (5 cm) from CO.

frost feather stockings

Schwäbische SOCKS

by **Lisa Stichweh**

Inspired by German twisted-stitch patterns, these socks begin with a woven design on the leg that transforms itself as it travels down the foot. Simple ribbing on the back of the leg continues down the heel, and an intricate gusset is incorporated in the top of the foot.

FINISHED SIZE About 7½ (8¼, 9)" (19 [21, 23] cm) foot circumference and 8½ (9, 9½)" (21.5 [23, 24] cm) foot length from back of heel to tip of toe. Foot length is adjustable. Socks shown measure 8¼" (21 cm) foot circumference.

YARN Fingering weight (#1 Super Fine). *Shown here:* Plymouth Yarn Happy Feet (90% superwash merino, 10% nylon; 192 yd [176 m]/1¾ oz [50 g]): #1249 maroon, 2 (2, 3) skeins.

NEEDLES U.S. size 1½ (2.5 mm): set of five double-pointed (dpn), two circular (cir), or one long cir. *Adjust needle size if necessary to obtain the correct gauge.*

NOTIONS Markers (m); cable needle (cn); tapestry needle.

GAUGE 30 sts and 48 rnds = 4" (10 cm) in St st.

notes

- To accommodate different methods of working—double-pointed needles, two circulars, or one long circular—the stitches are divided into two halves, which are referred to as "instep" and "heel" stitches. "Instep" stitches cover the top of the foot and the front of the leg; these stitches are on the first of two double-pointed needles, first of two circular needles, or first half of one long circular needle. "Heel" stitches cover the bottom of the foot, the heel, and the back of the leg; these stitches are on the last two double-pointed needles, the second of two circular needles, or second half of one long circular needle.

Cuff

Loosely CO 64 (70, 76) sts. Place marker (pm) and join for working in rnds, being careful not to twist sts.

Size 7½" (19 cm) only

NEXT RND: P1, [k1 through back loop (k1tbl)] 2 times, p1, k1tbl, pm, work Rib chart, pm, *k1tbl, p1, k1tbl; rep from * to last st, k1tbl.

Skip to All Sizes.

Size 8¼" (21 cm) only

NEXT RND: *K1 through back loop (k1tbl), p1, k1tbl; rep from * once more, pm, work Rib chart, pm, *k1tbl, p1, k1tbl; rep from * to end.

Skip to All Sizes.

Size 9" (23 cm) only

NEXT RND: P1, k1 through back loop (k1tbl), *k1tbl, p1, k1tbl; rep from * once more, pm, work Rib chart, pm, *k1tbl, p1, k1tbl; rep from * to last st, k1tbl.

All sizes

Rep last rnd 11 more times.

Leg

NEXT RND: Work in patt to m, work Leg Set-up chart to m, work in patt to end.

Cont in patt through Row 24 of chart.

NEXT RND: Work in patt to m, work Leg chart to m, work in patt to end.

Cont in patt through Row 24 of Leg chart.

Gusset

NEXT RND: Work in patt to m, work Gusset chart (page 126) to LLPI (see Glossary), work inc using purl st from cable (picking up leg needed for inc from behind work), work RLPI (see Glossary) as foll: beg next cable by sl 2 sts onto cn and hold in front, work RLPI using purl st on left needle, complete cable as usual, work to end of chart, sl m, work in patt to end—66 (72, 78) sts.

Cont in patt through Row 33 (35, 39) of chart, ending 2 sts before end of rnd on last rnd—98 (106, 116) sts.

Turn Heel

Heel is worked back and forth over last 32 (36, 38) sts of rnd; first 66 (70, 78) sts of rnd will be worked later for sole flap and instep. Shape heel using short-rows (see Glossary) as foll:

SET-UP RND: (RS) Wrap next st, turn work.

SHORT-ROW 1: (WS) P28 (32, 34), wrap next st, turn.

SHORT-ROW 2: Knit to 1 st before previously wrapped st, wrap next st, turn.

SHORT-ROW 3: Purl to 1 st before previously wrapped st, wrap next st, turn.

Rep last 2 short-rows 8 (9, 10) more times—10 (11, 12) wrapped sts at each side, 10 (12, 12) sts at center between wrapped sts, 1 unwrapped st at each end.

NEXT ROW: Knit to wrapped st, *work wrap tog with wrapped st; rep from * 8 (9, 10) more times, knit wrap, wrapped st, and last st (3 loops total) tog—97 (105, 115) sts rem.

Leg Set-up

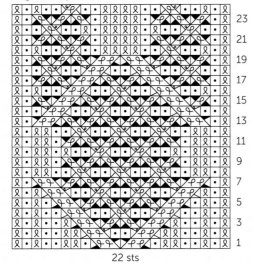

22 sts

Leg

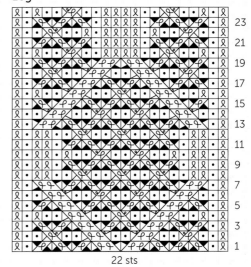

22 sts

Rib

| ℓ | • | ℓ | ℓ | • | • | ℓ | ℓ | ℓ | ℓ | • | • | ℓ | ℓ | ℓ | • | • | ℓ | ℓ | • | ℓ | ℓ | 1

22 sts

Sole Flap

SET-UP ROW 1: Work to m, remove m, work Row 34 (36, 40) of Gusset chart to m, remove m, work 5 (6, 8) sts, knit next st, wrap, and wrapped st (3 loops total) tog, *work wrap tog with wrapped st; rep from * 8 (9, 10) more times, k19 (22, 23), ssk, turn—95 (103, 113) sts rem.

SET-UP ROW 2: (WS) Sl 1 pwise with yarn in front (wyf), p28 (32, 34), p2tog, turn—94 (102, 112) sts rem.

ROW 1: Sl 1 pwise with yarn in back (wyb), k28 (32, 34), ssk, turn—1 st dec'd.

ROW 2: Sl 1 pwise wyf, p28 (32, 34), p2tog, turn—1 st dec'd.

Rep last 2 rows 14 (15, 17) more times—64 (70, 76) sts rem.

NEXT RND: (RS) Sl 1 pwise wyb, k28 (32, 34), ssk, k8 (9, 11), pm, work Row 3 (1, 1) of Foot chart (page 126), pm, k8 (9, 11), pm for end of instep, k2tog, k29 (33, 35), pm for beg of rnd—62 (68, 74) sts rem: 32 (34, 38) sts for instep, 30 (34, 36) sts for sole.

	k
•	p
ℓ	k1tbl
V	RLI (see Glossary)
⅃	LLI (see Glossary)
↖	RLPI (see Glossary)
↗	LLPI (see Glossary)
▨	no stitch

sl 1 st onto cn, hold in back, k1tbl, k1tbl from cn

sl 1 st onto cn, hold in front, k1tbl, k1tbl from cn

sl 1 st onto cn, hold in back, k1tbl, p1 from cn

sl 1 st onto cn, hold in front, p1, k1tbl from cn

sl 1 st onto cn, hold in back, [k1tbl] 2 times, k1tbl from cn

sl 2 sts onto cn, hold in front, k1tbl, [k1tbl] 2 times from cn

sl 1 st onto cn, hold in back, [k1tbl] 2 times, p1 from cn

sl 2 sts onto cn, hold in front, p1, [k1tbl] 2 times from cn

schwäbische socks

Gusset

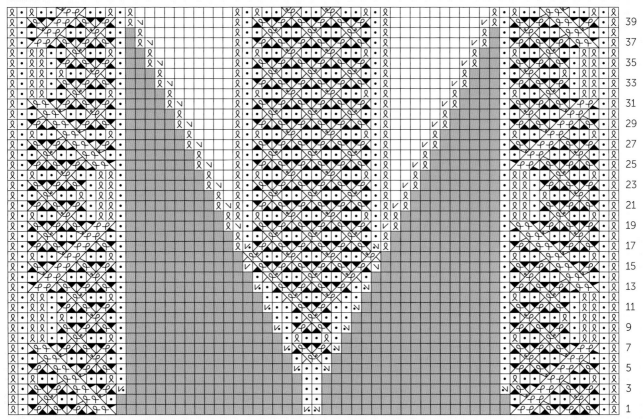

39
37
35
33
31
29
27
25
23
21
19
17
15
13
11
9
7
5
3
1

Foot

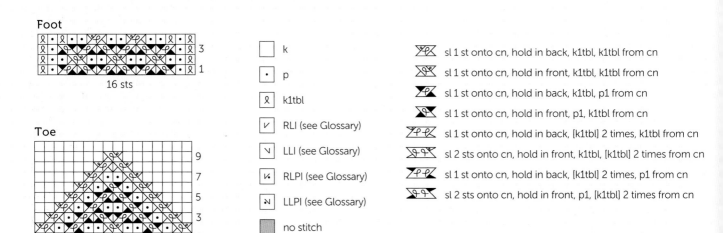

3
1

16 sts

Toe

9
7
5
3
1

16 sts

	k
•	p
ℓ	k1tbl
V	RLI (see Glossary)
⅄	LLI (see Glossary)
↖	RLPI (see Glossary)
↘	LLPI (see Glossary)
	no stitch

sl 1 st onto cn, hold in back, k1tbl, k1tbl from cn

sl 1 st onto cn, hold in front, k1tbl, k1tbl from cn

sl 1 st onto cn, hold in back, k1tbl, p1 from cn

sl 1 st onto cn, hold in front, p1, k1tbl from cn

sl 1 st onto cn, hold in back, [k1tbl] 2 times, k1tbl from cn

sl 2 sts onto cn, hold in front, k1tbl, [k1tbl] 2 times from cn

sl 1 st onto cn, hold in back, [k1tbl] 2 times, p1 from cn

sl 2 sts onto cn, hold in front, p1, [k1tbl] 2 times from cn

Foot

Work even in patt as established until piece measures 5¼ (5½, 6)" (13.5 [14, 15] cm) from back of heel, or 3¼ (3½, 3½)" (8.5 [9, 9] cm) less than desired finished length, ending with Row 4 of Foot chart.

NEXT RND: Work to m, work Toe chart to m, work to end.

Cont in patt through Row 10 of chart, removing chart m on last rnd.

Work in St st until piece measures 7 (7¼, 7¾)" (18 [18.5, 19.5] cm) from back of heel, or 1½ (1¾, 1¾)" (3.8 [4.5, 4.5] cm) less than desired finished length.

Toe

SET-UP RND: K1, [ssk] 1 (0, 1) time, knit to 3 sts before m, [k2tog] 1 (0, 1) time, knit to end—60 (68, 72) sts rem: 30 (34, 36) sts each for instep and sole.

RND 1: *K1, ssk, knit to 3 sts before m, k2tog, k1; rep from * once more—4 sts dec'd.

RND 2: Knit.

Rep last 2 rnds 6 (7, 7) more times—32 (36, 40) sts rem. Rep Rnd 1 only 3 (3, 4) times—20 (24, 24) sts rem. Cut yarn, leaving a 12" (30.5 cm) tail.

Finishing

With tail threaded on a tapestry needle, use Kitchener st (see Glossary) to graft sts tog. Weave in loose ends. Block lightly.

schwäbische socks

top (down) toes

by Kate Atherley

Although most patterns use the same toe, you can customize your top-down socks for better fit.

There are many versions of the top-down sock toe: some pointy, some square, some round; some short, some long; some that require grafting, some that don't. There are five main variables that control the shape and length of a toe.

Let's look at how each of these factors changes the shape of your sock toes. (Keep in mind that all of these examples assume that the start of the round is at the center of the sole stitches.)

NUMBER OF DECREASES PER ROUND

Most common toe shaping decreases four stitches per round, but working six or eight decreases at a time—like a classic hat crown—creates a rounder toe.

POSITION OF DECREASES

The wedge toe places four decreases at the sides of the foot, two stitches apart. The star toe places four decreases distributed evenly around the sock.

DIRECTION OF DECREASES

If all the decreases are the same—the right-leaning k2tog or the left-leaning ssk—as in the star toe, an elegant spiral results. The wedge toe and flat toe use a left-leaning decrease on the right side and a right-leaning decrease on the left side to create curves in toward the center of the toe.

FREQUENCY OF DECREASES

The length and the angle of the toe are determined by how frequently stitches are decreased. Working only decrease rounds creates a 45° angle, too steep for the average foot. Decreasing less frequently (e.g., every second or third round) creates a longer toe at a less steep angle; changing the rate of decrease (slow at first, faster at the end) creates a more natural curved shape. In one classic method (which I'll call "half and half"), the first half of the decreases alternate with even rounds, while the second half are worked without plain rows between.

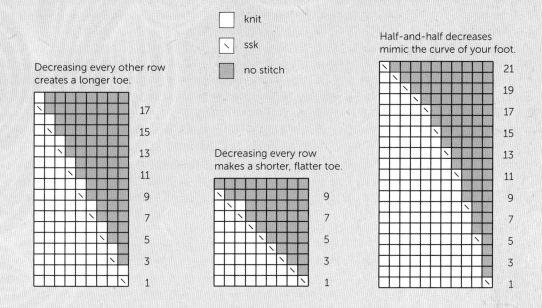

Decreasing every other row creates a longer toe.

knit

ssk

no stitch

Decreasing every row makes a shorter, flatter toe.

Half-and-half decreases mimic the curve of your foot.

NUMBER OF STITCHES LEFT AT THE END

For a flatter, wider toe, stop decreasing earlier; for a pointier, longer toe, work more decrease rounds. A toe ending with only eight to twelve stitches is best closed up by running the yarn through the final stitches and pulling snug. A toe that finishes with more than twelve stitches is best grafted.

These factors can be combined in many ways, although some combinations are more successful than others! Decreasing every other round down to a small number of stitches yields a very pointy toe. A more gradual decrease pattern, as in the star toe or barn toe, creates a much better shape. If you decrease every round to a larger number of stitches, you'll get a very short and flat toe, ideal for a very wide foot with short toes (if you're good at grafting).

top (down) toes

Wedge Toe

Star Toe

Round Toe

Barn Toe

Toes in Practice

Try these toe patterns on for size—or find your own combination of decrease and even rounds until you find your perfect fit.

WEDGE TOE

DECREASE RND: Knit to 3 sts before instep, k2tog, k2, ssk, knit to 3 sts before end of instep, k2tog, k2, ssk, knit to end of rnd—4 sts dec'd.

Alternate even and decrease rnds until about one-third of the original number of sts rem. Graft closed.

A wider version can be created by placing the decreases farther away from the edges:

DECREASE RND: Knit to 4 sts before instep, k2tog, k4, ssk, knit to 4 sts before end of instep, k2tog, k4, ssk, knit to end of rnd—4 sts dec'd.

A flatter toe uses a double decrease centered on the sides:

DECREASE RND: Knit to 1 st before instep, sl, k1, p2sso (see Glossary), knit to 1 st before end of instep, sl, k1, p2sso, knit to end of rnd—4 sts dec'd.

STAR TOE

DECREASE RND: Knit to 2 sts before instep, k2tog, knit to 2 sts before center of instep, k2tog, knit to 2 sts before end of instep, k2tog, knit to 2 sts before end of rnd, k2tog.

Left and Right

Alternate decrease and even rnds until about half the desired decreases have been worked, then work only decrease rnds until 8–10 sts rem. Pass the tail of yarn through the remaining stitches and pull tight to close the hole.

ROUND TOE

More decreases worked less often make the decrease lines less visible. You'll need a multiple of 8 stitches.

DECREASE RND 1: *K6, k2tog, place marker (pm); rep from * to end.

Work 2 rounds even.

DECREASE RND 2: *Knit to 2 sts before m, k2tog; rep from * to end.

Work decrease round 2 every 3rd round until eight or ten sts rem. Pass tail through rem sts and pull tight to close the hole.

BARN TOE

This is my favorite toe. It's a bit longer than a standard wedge toe and requires no grafting. It uses the same decrease round as the wedge toe but varies the number of even rounds between.

DECREASE RND: Knit to 3 sts before instep, k2tog, k2, ssk, knit to 3 sts before end of instep, k2tog, k2, ssk, knit to end of rnd—4 sts dec'd.

Work 3 rnds even.

*Work decrease rnd, then work 2 rnds even. Rep from * 1 more time.

**Work decrease rnd, then work 1 rnd even. Rep from ** 2 more times.

Work decrease rnd until 8 or 10 sts rem. Pass tail through rem sts and pull tight to close the hole.

LEFT AND RIGHT

The majority of sock toes are symmetrical, but there's no reason they have to be. When working a wedge toe, use the barn toe shaping on the big-toe side and the "half and half" shaping progression (as in the Star Toe) on the other side. This creates a shape that is roomier close to the big toe and more angled on the outside of the foot. The peak of the toe sits off-center, which better conforms to the shape of most feet.

top (down) toes

Our Paths Cross
SOCKS

by **Lorilee Beltman**

For practical purposes, this is a simple toe-up stockinette stitch sock, but the vertically carried strands make it anything but plain. The Pyramid Heel, with decreases at the back of the foot, provides a comfortable fit and an attractive Eye-of-Partridge pattern. Wear them with clogs and blaze a trail.

FINISHED SIZE About 7 (7½, 8)" (18 [19, 20.5] cm) foot circumference and 7¾ (8, 8½)" (19.5 [20.5, 21.5] cm) foot length from bottom of heel to top of cuff. Foot length is adjustable.

YARN Fingering weight (Super Fine #1). *Shown here:* Plucky Knitter Primo Fingering (70% merino, 25% cashmere, 5% nylon; 385 yd [352 m]/100 g): barely birch (MC), 1 (1, 2) skein(s); sticky toffee (CC1) and bohemian blue (CC2), 16 yd (14.5 m) each.

NEEDLES U.S. size 1 (2.25 mm): set of five double-pointed (dpn), two circular (cir), or one long cir. *Adjust needle size if necessary to obtain the correct gauge.*

NOTIONS Markers (m); waste yarn; tapestry needle.

GAUGE 34 sts and 50 rnds = 4" (10 cm) in St st.

stitch guide

ALTERNATIVE METHOD TO PURL THROUGH BACK LOOP (P1TBL)

Insert right needle in purl st as usual, but wrap yarn in the opposite direction (clockwise instead of counterclockwise). The new st will be turned on the needle (right leg in back). On the next rnd, work this st through the front loop to create a twisted purl st, and again wrap the yarn clockwise. This maneuver gives the same result as purling through the back loop but is easier to accomplish.

EYE-OF-PARTRIDGE STITCH
(multiple of 2 sts)

RND 1: *Sl 1 purlwise (pwise) with yarn in back (wyb), k1; rep from *.

RNDS 2 AND 4: Knit.

RND 3: *K1, sl 1 pwise wyb; rep from *.

Rep Rnds 1–4 for patt.

notes

✖ To accommodate different methods of working—double-pointed needles, two circulars, or one long circular—the stitches are divided into two halves, which are referred to as "instep" and "heel" stitches. "Instep" stitches cover the top of the foot and the front of the leg; these stitches are on the first of two double-pointed needles, first of two circular needles, or first half of one long circular needle. "Heel" stitches cover the bottom of the foot, the heel, and the back of the leg; these stitches are on the last two double-pointed needles, the second of two circular needles, or second half of one long circular needle.

✖ See page 137 for instructions on vertical stranding.

✖ These socks are toe-up with a sole flap and pyramid gusset. This construction places all gusset decreases at the back of the heel, forming a pyramid shape from the heel turn that ends in a point at the top of the heel. The resulting sock has heel shaping at the actual heel and a smooth, uninterrupted front surface for patterning.

✖ Reverse the positions of the contrasting color (CC) paths on the second sock to make a mirrored pair.

Toe

With MC and leaving a 12" (30.5 cm) tail over left forefinger, use Judy's Magic method (see Glossary) to CO 4 sts over 2 ends of cir needle (or 2 needles)—2 sts on each needle.

RND 1: Holding tail tog with working yarn, knit—4 sts worked with doubled yarn.

Drop tail and hold to RS of work; tail serves as beg-of-rnd m.

RND 2: With single strand of working yarn, knit each strand of doubled-yarn sts separately—8 sts.

RND 3: *K1, LLI (see Glossary), RLI (see Glossary), k1; rep from * 3 more times—16 sts.

RNDS 4 AND 5: Knit.

RND 6: *K2, LLI, RLI, k2; rep from * 3 more times—24 sts.

RNDS 7 AND 8: Knit.

RND 9: *K3, LLI, RLI, k3; rep from * 3 more times—32 sts.

RNDS 10–12: Knit.

RND 13: *K4, LLI, RLI, k4; rep from * 3 more times—40 sts.

RNDS 14–16: Knit.

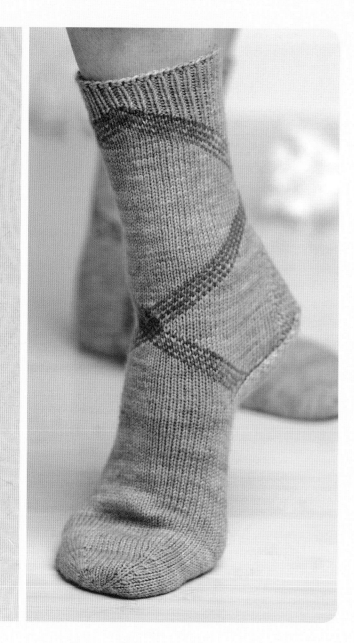

Sizes 7½ (8)" (19 [20.5] cm) only

RND 26: *K7, LLI, RLI, k7; rep from * 3 more times—64 sts: 32 sts for instep, 32 sts for sole.

Skip to Foot.

Size 8" (20.5 cm) only

RNDS 27–30: Knit.

RND 31: *K8, LLI, RLI, k8; rep from * once more, k32—68 sts: 36 sts for instep, 32 sts for sole.

Foot

Work even in St st until piece measures 3½" (9 cm) less than desired finished length to back of heel.

Heel

SOLE FLAP

The sole flap is worked back and forth on 32 sole sts; rem sts will be worked later for instep. Turn work.

SET-UP ROW: (WS) P32, turn.

ROW 1: (RS) *Sl 1 purlwise (pwise) with yarn in back (wyb), k1; rep from * to end, turn.

ROW 2: (WS) Sl 1 pwise with yarn in front (wyf), purl to end, turn.

ROW 3: (RS) Sl 1 pwise wyb, k2, *sl 1 pwise wyb, k1; rep from * to last st, k1, turn.

ROW 4: (WS) Sl 1 pwise wyf, purl to end, turn.

Rep Rows 1–4 ten more times, then work Row 1 once more—flap measures about 2½" (6.5 cm), with 23 chain-edge sts along each selvedge.

HEEL TURN

note: Eye-of-partridge st cont through heel turn.

ROW 1: (WS) Sl 1, p17, ssp (see Glossary), p1, turn.

ROW 2: (RS) Sl 1, k2, sl 1, k1, sl 1, k2tog, k1, turn.

ROW 3: Sl 1, p6, ssp, p1, turn.

ROW 4: Sl 1, k2, [sl 1, k1] 2 times, sl 1, k2tog, k1, turn.

ROW 5: Sl 1, p8, ssp, p1, turn.

ROW 6: Sl 1, k2, [sl 1, k1] 3 times, sl 1, k2tog, k1, turn.

ROW 7: Sl 1, p10, ssp, p1, turn.

ROW 8: Sl 1, k2, [sl 1, k1] 4 times, sl 1, k2tog, k1, turn.

ROW 9: Sl 1, p12, ssp, p1, turn.

RND 17: *K5, LLI, RLI, k5; rep from * 3 more times—48 sts.

RNDS 18–20: Knit.

RND 21: *K6, LLI, RLI, k6; rep from * 3 more times—56 sts: 28 sts for instep, 28 sts for sole.

RNDS 22–25: Knit.

Size 7" (18 cm) only

RND 26: K28, *k7, LLI, RLI, k7; rep from * once more—60 sts: 28 sts for instep, 32 sts for sole.

Skip to Foot.

ROW 10: Sl 1, k2, [sl 1, k1] 5 times, sl 1, k2tog, k1, turn.

ROW 11: Sl 1, p14, ssp, p1, turn.

ROW 12: Sl 1, k2, [sl 1, k1] 6 times, sl 1, k2tog, k1, turn.

ROW 13: Sl 1, p16, ssp, turn.

ROW 14: K2, [sl 1, k1] 7 times, sl 1, k2tog—18 heel sts rem. Do not turn.

PYRAMID HEEL GUSSET

NEXT RND: (RS; set-up rnd) Place marker (pm), pick up and knit (see Glossary) 24 sts along left edge of sole flap, k28 (32, 36) instep sts, pick up and knit 24 sts along right edge of sole flap, knit to m—94 (98, 102) sts total.

NEXT RND: Remove m, k9, pm for end of gusset, k59 (63, 67), pm for beg of gusset (also beg of rnd)—35 pyramid heel gusset sts, 59 (63, 67) leg sts.

DECREASE SECTION

RND 1: (dec rnd) Ssk, work eye-of-partridge st (see Stitch Guide) to 2 sts before m, k2tog, work Crossing chart (pages 138–140) for your size, working vertical stranding as described on page 137—2 sts dec'd.

RNDS 2 AND 3: K1tbl, work eye-of-partridge st to 1 st before m, k1; work next rnd of Crossing chart.

Rep Rnds 1–3 fourteen more times, then work Rnds 1 and 2 once more—62 (66, 70) sts rem; 3 gusset sts between markers.

NEXT RND: (inc rnd; Row 48 of chart) Work 3 gusset sts as for Rnd 3, work in patt as established to end of rnd—63 (67, 71) sts.

NEXT RND: (dec rnd) Sl 2 as if to k2tog, k1, p2sso (see Glossary), remove end-of-gusset m, work in patt to end—61 (65, 69) sts rem.

NEXT RND: Work Row 50 of chart over all sts.

Leg

Work in patt as established to end of chart—62 (66, 70) sts.

Using Jeny's Surprisingly Stretchy method (see Glossary), BO all sts.

Finishing

With yarn threaded on a tapestry needle, weave in MC ends. With WS facing, untie rem CC yarn. With 1 CC strand threaded on a tapestry needle, weave strand into channel it has formed on WS for about 1" (2.5 cm); trim. Rep for rem CC strands. Block flat.

VERTICAL STRANDING

These socks are created with Lorilee's vertical stranding technique, which allows the pattern stitches to be worked in contrasting-color yarns without carrying them across the back of the entire work.

INTRODUCING CC STRANDS

For each sock, cut two 4 yd (3.7 m) lengths of each contrasting color (CC).

*On Round 1 of chart, fold the yarn in half and knit first CC stitch from the middle of the strand. Drop the strand. With MC, knit one stitch. With CC, knit next stitch, also from the middle of the folded strand just used. Drop the strand; do not twine the yarns on the back of the work. With MC, knit one stitch.

Repeat from * for the next two CC stitches; four CC stitches have been introduced, and four strands of CC yarn hang at the back of the work.

Repeat for CC2.

MANAGING CC STRANDS

Before working Round 2, stop for yarn management: Use your fingers to comb each CC strand even and parallel. Trim the far ends even. Holding all strands together and beginning close to the work, wrap the strands in a figure eight (as for a yarn butterfly), then wrap the ends around the figure eight and tie about three half hitches to secure. Using a length of waste yarn, tie the center of the figure eight firmly.

As the chart is worked, pull out one loop at a time from the figure eight as needed.

WORKING CC STITCHES

Each vertically stranded CC stitch is knitted with its own strand; a strand is never used to knit more than one stitch in any rnd. Unlike typical stranded knitting, contrasting yarns are not carried across the round at the back of the work. There are a few things to remember when knitting with vertical stranding:

When using MC to knit into an existing CC stitch that is a part of a vertical strand that is moving to the left, no special treatment is needed; knit as usual.

When using MC to knit into an existing CC stitch that is a part of a vertical strand moving to the right, knit it through the back loop.

Note: In this case, knitting through the back loop does not result in a twisted stitch. Because the yarn is coming from the left, the stitch must be knitted through the back loop in order to be open.

When creating a CC stitch, hold the MC off to the left. From the right, pick up the strand of CC yarn attached to that stripe and knit as usual, then drop the CC strand.

Reposition stitches as needed to avoid dividing a color section between needles.

Crossing, size 8"

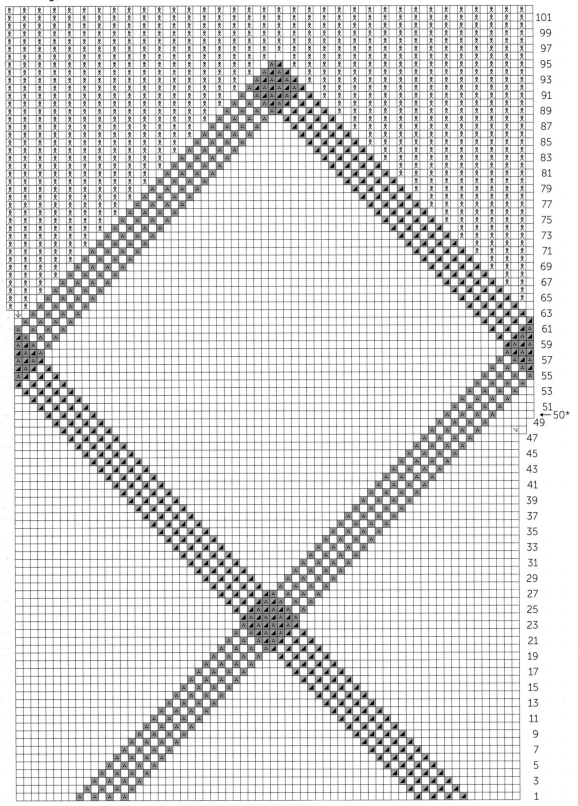

* *Work as given in directions*

□	knit with MC
⁙	knit with CC1
◪	knit with CC2
ℐ	purl tbl (pltbl)
﹀	LLI
↯	k1f&b

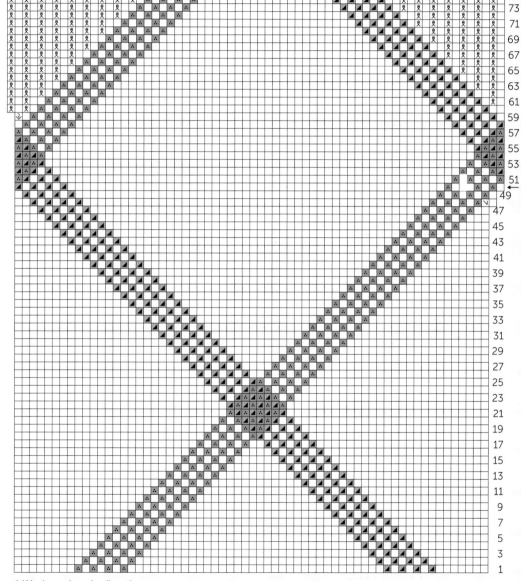

* Work as given in directions

Crossing, size 7"

knit with MC

knit with CC1

knit with CC2

purl tbl (pltbl)

LLI

k1f&b

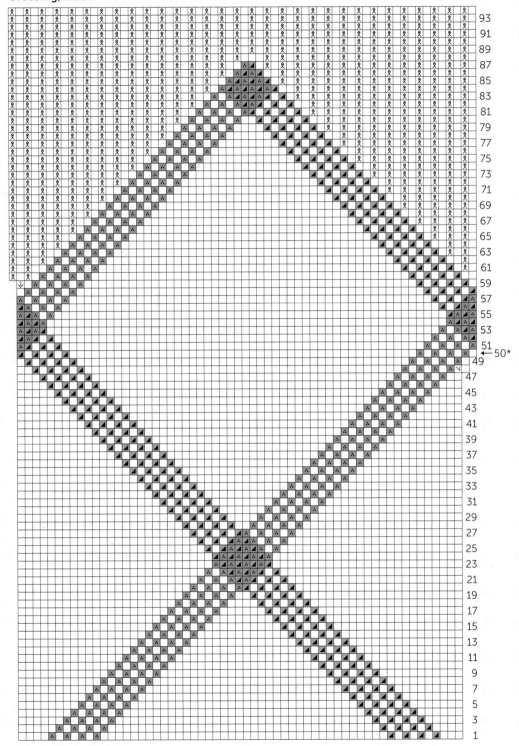

93
91
89
87
85
83
81
79
77
75
73
71
69
67
65
63
61
59
57
55
53
51
←50*
49
47
45
43
41
39
37
35
33
31
29
27
25
23
21
19
17
15
13
11
9
7
5
3
1

Work as given in directions

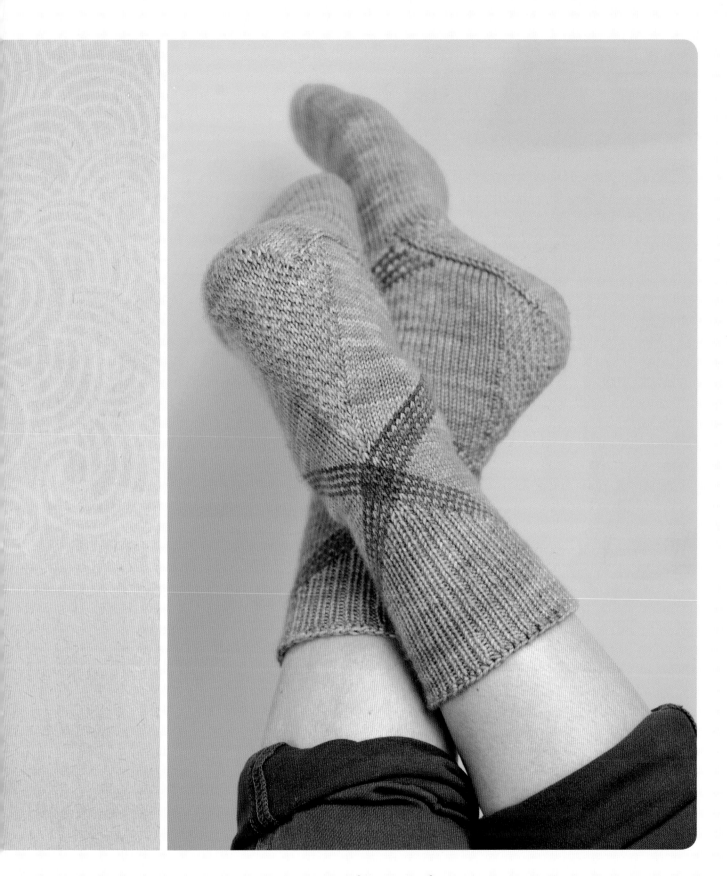

our paths cross socks

Passerine SOCKS

by **Cookie A**

The design of these socks evokes the structure of feathers, with sleek vanes and prominent quills coming together in the classic interlocking arrangement. Twisted-stitch ribbing alternates with stockinette to create a three-dimensional design, and two different methods of decreasing taper the feathers. Let your fingers fly through this addictive pattern!

FINISHED SIZE About 8" (20.5 cm) foot circumference and 8¾" (22 cm) foot length from back of heel to tip of toe. Foot length is adjustable.

YARN Fingering weight (#1 Super Fine). *Shown here:* Blue Moon Fiber Arts Socks that Rock Lightweight (100% superwash merino; 360 yd [329 m]/127 g): spinel (blue), 1 skein.

NEEDLES U.S. size 1½ (2.5 mm): set of five double-pointed (dpn), two circular (cir), or one long cir. *Adjust needle size if necessary to obtain the correct gauge.*

NOTIONS Markers (m); tapestry needle.

GAUGE 34 sts and 44 rnds = 4" (10 cm) in charted patt; 30 sts and 44 rnds = 4" (10 cm) in St st.

notes

✱ To accommodate different methods of working—double-pointed needles, two circulars, or one long circular—the stitches are divided into two halves, which are referred to as "instep" and "heel" stitches. "Instep" stitches cover the top of the foot and the front of the leg; these stitches are on the first of two double-pointed needles, first of two circular needles, or first half of one long circular needle. "Heel" stitches cover the bottom of the foot, the heel, and the back of the leg; these stitches are on the last two double-pointed needles, the second of two circular needles, or second half of one long circular needle.

✱ These socks are worked top-down with a traditional slip-stitch heel.

Leg

CO 64 sts. Distribute sts over needles so each needle holds a multiple of 16 sts. Place marker (pm) if needed and join for working in rnds, being careful not to twist sts.

NEXT RND: *K1tbl, p1; rep from * around.

Cont in twisted rib until piece measures 1" (2.5 cm) from CO.

Work Rows 1–14 of Set-up chart once. Work Rows 1–28 of Feather chart once, then work Rows 1–14 once more—piece measures about 6" (15 cm) from CO.

Heel

HEEL FLAP

Heel flap is worked back and forth on first 31 sts of rnd; last 33 sts of rnd will be worked later for instep.

ROW 1: (RS) [Sl 1 purlwise (pwise) with yarn in back (wyb), k1] 15 times, k1, turn.

ROW 2: (WS) Sl 1 pwise with yarn in front (wyf), p30, turn.

Rep last 2 rows until heel flap measures 2¼" (5.5 cm), ending with a WS row.

TURN HEEL

ROW 1: (RS) Sl 1 pwise wyb, k17, ssk, k1, turn work.

ROW 2: (WS) Sl 1 pwise wyf, p6, p2tog, p1, turn.

ROW 3: Sl 1 pwise wyb, knit to 1 st before gap, ssk (1 st from each side of gap), k1, turn.

ROW 4: Sl 1 pwise wyf, purl to 1 st before gap, p2tog (1 st from each side of gap), p1, turn.

Rep last 2 rows 4 more times—19 sts rem for heel.

SHAPE GUSSETS

NEXT ROW: (RS) Sl 1 pwise wyb, k8, pm for beg of rnd, k10 heel sts, pick up and knit (see Glossary) 1 st in each sl st along edge of heel flap, M1 (see Glossary), pm to mark right side of foot, work 33 instep sts in established patt, pm to mark left side of foot, M1, pick up and knit 1 st in each sl st along edge of heel flap (picking up same number of sts as on other edge of heel flap), knit to end of rnd.

Right and left side markers divide foot into instep and sole.

Set-up

13
11
9
7
5
3
1

	k
•	p
Ω	k1tbl
o	yo
/	k2tog
\	ssk
⋏	sl 1, k2tog, psso
∧	sl 2 as if to k2tog, k1, p2sso
	pattern repeat

Feather

27
25
23
21
19
17
15
13
11
9
7
5
3
1

RND 1: Knit to 2 sts before right side m, k2tog, work in patt to left side m, sl m, ssk, knit to end—2 sts dec'd.

RND 2: Work even in patt, working sole in St st.

Rep last 2 rnds until 64 sts rem: 33 instep sts, 31 sole sts.

Foot

Work even in patt until foot measures 6¾" (17 cm) from back of heel, or 2" (5 cm) less than desired finished length.

Toe

Knit to right side m—this is new beg of rnd.

RND 1: K2tog, k29, ssk, knit to end of rnd—62 sts rem: 31 sts each for instep and sole.

RND 2: Knit.

RND 3: K1, ssk, knit to 3 sts before left side m, k2tog, k1, sl m, k1, ssk, knit to 3 sts before right side m, k2tog, k1—4 sts dec'd.

Rep last 2 rnds 9 more times—22 sts rem.

Finishing

Graft toe with Kitchener st (see Glossary). Weave in loose ends. Block as desired.

Escadaria SOCKS

by **Kristi Geraci**

Named for the Portuguese word for "stairway," these socks feature a pattern that climbs slowly across the foot and upward in a grid pattern that gives way to a smocked ribbing pattern. The movement of the motif makes these intriguing in solid yarn and a perfect complement to handpainted yarn. Toe-up construction is paired with a flap-and-gusset heel; substitute a short-row heel if you prefer to keep the stitch count constant for a multicolored yarn.

FINISHED SIZE About 7½ (9, 10½)" (19 [23, 26.5] cm) foot and leg circumference. Foot length is adjustable. Socks shown measure 9" (23 cm) foot circumference.

YARN Fingering weight (Super fine #1). *Shown here:* Lorna's Laces Shepherd Sock (80% superwash wool, 20% nylon; 435 yd [400 m]/100 g): roadside gerry (variegated) or harvest (semi-solid), 1 skein.

NEEDLES U.S. size 1 (2.25 mm): set of five double-pointed (dpn), two circular (cir), or one long cir. *Adjust needle size if necessary to obtain the correct gauge.*

NOTIONS Markers (m); tapestry needle.

GAUGE 32 sts and 48 rnds = 4" (10 cm) in St st.

stitch guide

WRAPPED STITCH
(worked over 3 sts)

Pass 3rd st on left needle over 1st and 2nd sts and off needle, then k1, M1, k1.

notes

✱ To accommodate different methods of working—double-pointed needles, two circulars, or one long circular—the stitches are divided into two halves, which are referred to as "instep" and "heel" stitches. "Instep" stitches cover the top of the foot and the front of the leg; these stitches are on the first of two double-pointed needles, first of two circular needles, or first half of one long circular needle. "Heel" stitches cover the bottom of the foot, the heel, and the back of the leg; these stitches are on the last two double-pointed needles, the second of two circular needles, or second half of one long circular needle.

✱ These socks are worked from the toe up.

✱ Left and right socks are mirror images of one another.

Left Sock

TOE

Using Judy's Magic method (see Glossary) or your favorite toe-up method, CO 24 sts. Place marker (pm) and join for working in rnds.

NEXT RND: K12 (for instep), pm, k12 (for sole).

INC RND: *K1, M1 (see Glossary), knit to 1 st before m, M1, k1; rep from * once more—4 sts inc'd.

Rep Inc rnd every other rnd 8 (11, 14) more times—60 (72, 84) sts.

FOOT

note: Gusset shaping beg when sock measures 3½" (9 cm) less than desired finished length to back of heel and is worked at the same time as the instep sts. Read through the foll instructions before proceeding.

RNDS 1–10: K24 (30, 36), work 6 sts of Left chart A (page 150) once, knit to end of rnd.

RNDS 11–20: K18 (24, 30), work 6 sts of Left Chart A once, work 6 sts of Left Chart B (page 150) once, knit to end of rnd.

RNDS 21–30: K12 (18, 24), work 6 sts of Left Chart A once, work 6 sts of Left Chart B 2 times, knit to end of rnd.

RNDS 31–40: K6 (12, 18), work 6 sts of Left Chart A once, work 6 sts of Left Chart B 2 times, work 6 sts of Left Chart C (page 150) once, knit to end of rnd.

RNDS 41–49: K0 (6, 12), work 6 sts of Left Chart A once, work 6 sts of Left Chart B 2 times, work 6 sts of Left Chart C once, k3, p3, knit to end of rnd.

Size 7½" (19 cm) only

RND 50: Work 6 sts of Left Chart A once, work 6 sts of Left Chart B 2 times, M1P (see Glossary), work 6 sts of Left Chart C once, work wrapped st (see Stitch Guide) over 3 sts, p3, knit to end of rnd—31 instep sts.

For rem of sock to cuff, work instep sts as foll: Work 6 sts of Left Chart B 3 times, p1, work 12-st rep of Left Chart D (page 150) once. Skip to Shape Gussets.

Size 10½" (26.5 cm) only

RND 60: Work 6 sts of Left Chart A once, work 6 sts of Left Chart B twice, work 6 sts of Left Chart C once, work wrapped st over 3 sts, p3, k3, p3, knit to end of rnd.

RNDS 61–69: Work 6 sts of Left Chart A once, work 6 sts of Left Chart B 2 times, work 6 sts of Left Chart C once, [k3, p3] 3 times, knit to end of rnd.

RND 70: Work 6 sts of Left Chart A once, work 6 sts of Left Chart B 2 times, M1P (see Glossary), work 6 sts of Left Chart C once, work wrapped st over 3 sts, p3, k3, p3, work wrapped st over 3 sts, p3, knit to end of rnd—43 instep sts.

For rem of sock to cuff, work instep sts as foll: Work 6 sts of Left Chart B 3 times, p1, work 12-st rep of Left Chart D 2 times.

SHAPE GUSSETS

At the same time, when sock measures 3½" (9 cm) less than desired length to back of heel, shape gusset as foll:

INC RND: Work instep sts as directed, sl m, k1, M1, knit to last st, M1, k1—2 sts inc'd.

Work 1 rnd even.

Rep last 2 rnds 14 more times—60 (66, 72) sole sts.

TURN HEEL

Work heel turn back and forth using short-rows (see Glossary) as foll:

SHORT-ROW 1: (RS) Work instep sts to marker, k44 (50, 56), wrap next st, turn work.

SHORT-ROW 2: (WS) P28 (34, 40), wrap next st, turn.

SHORT-ROW 3: Knit to 1 st before wrapped st, wrap next st, turn.

SHORT-ROW 4: Purl to 1 st before wrapped st, wrap next st, turn.

Rep Rows 3 and 4 nine more times—11 sts wrapped on each side; 8 (14, 20) sts rem unwrapped in center of heel.

HEEL FLAP

SHORT-ROW 1: (RS) Sl 1 purlwise (pwise) with yarn in back (wyb), k17 (23, 29), working 10 wraps tog with wrapped sts, knit next wrap tog with wrapped st and next (3 loops total) on left needle, turn—1 gusset st dec'd.

Sizes 9 (10½)" (23 [26.5] cm) only

RND 50: K6 (12), work 6 sts of Left Chart A once, work 6 sts of Left Chart B 2 times, work 6 sts of Left Chart C once, work wrapped st (see Stitch Guide) over 3 sts, p3, knit to end of rnd.

RNDS 51–59: K0 (6), work 6 sts of Left Chart A once, work 6 sts of Left Chart B 2 times, work 6 sts of Left Chart C once, [k3, p3] 2 times, knit to end of rnd.

Cont for your size as foll:

Size 9" (23 cm) only

RND 60: Work 6 sts of Left Chart A once, work 6 sts of Left Chart B 2 times, M1P (see Glossary), work 6 sts of Left Chart C once, work wrapped st over 3 sts, p3, k3, p3, knit to end of rnd—37 instep sts.

For rem of sock to cuff, work instep sts as foll: Work 6 sts of Left Chart B 3 times, p1, work Left Chart D over 18 sts (12-st rep and last 6 sts of chart). Skip to Shape Gussets.

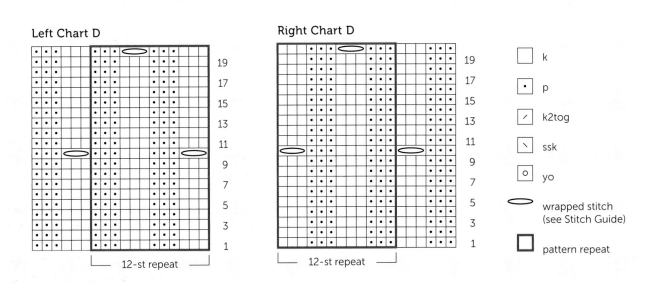

Left Chart A

Left Chart B

Left Chart C

Right Chart A

Right Chart B

Right Chart C

Left Chart D

12-st repeat

Right Chart D

12-st repeat

☐ k

• p

/ k2tog

\ ssk

o yo

⬭ wrapped stitch
(see Stitch Guide)

☐ pattern repeat

SHORT-ROW 2: (WS) Sl 1 pwise with yarn in front (wyf), p28 (34, 40), working 10 wraps tog with wrapped sts, ssp (see Glossary) next wrap tog with wrapped st and next st (3 loops total) on left needle, turn—1 gusset st dec'd.

SHORT-ROW 3: [Sl 1 pwise wyb, k1] 14 (17, 20) times, sl 1 pwise wyb, k2tog, turn—1 gusset st dec'd.

SHORT-ROW 4: Sl 1 wyf, p28 (31, 34), ssp, turn—1 gusset st dec'd.

Rep Rows 3 and 4 until 1 gusset st rem each side, ending with a WS row—63 (75, 87) sts: 32 (38, 44) heel sts, 31 (37, 43) instep sts.

Resume working in rnds as foll:

NEXT RND: [Sl 1 pwise wyb, k1] 15 (18, 21) times, for end of rnd, work gusset st tog with first instep st (removing m and keeping to instep patt as established), cont as established to last instep st, work last instep st tog with next gusset st (removing m and keeping to instep patt as established), cont working Left Chart D as established to end of rnd, M1—62 (74, 86) sts.

NEXT RND: Work 6 sts of Left Chart B 3 times, p1, work 12-st rep of Left Chart D 3 (4, 5) times, work last 6 sts of chart, k1.

Cont in patt as established until sock measures about 2" (5 cm) less than desired finished length, ending with Row 10 of Left Chart B.

CUFF

RND 1: Work 6 sts of Left Chart C 3 times, p1, work Left Chart D as established to last st, k1.

RND 2: Work 6 sts of Left Chart C 2 times, p4, k1, ssk, work Left Chart D to last st, k1—61 (73, 85) sts rem.

RNDS 3–8: Work 6 sts of Left Chart C 3 times, work Left Chart D to last st, k1.

RND 9: Work 6 sts of Left Chart C 3 times, work Left Chart D to last st, pm for new end of rnd.

RND 10: K2tog (removing m), k2, p3, work 6 sts of Left Chart C 2 times, work Left Chart D to end of rnd—60 (72, 84) sts rem.

NEXT RND: *K3, p3; rep from * around.

Rep last rnd until ribbing measures 1" (2.5 cm). BO in patt.

Right Sock

TOE

Using Judy's Magic CO or your favorite toe-up method, CO 24 sts. Pm and join for working in rnds.

NEXT RND: K12 for instep, pm, k12 for sole.

INC RND: *K1, M1, knit to 1 st before m, M1, k1; rep from * once more—4 sts inc'd.

Rep Inc rnd every other rnd 8 (11, 14) more times— 60 (72, 84) sts.

FOOT

note: Gusset shaping beg when sock measures 3½" (9 cm) less than desired length to back of heel and is worked at the same time as the instep sts. Read through the foll instructions before proceeding.

RNDS 1–10: Work 6 sts of Right Chart A once, knit to end of rnd.

RNDS 11–20: Work 6 sts of Right Chart B once, work 6 sts of Right Chart A once, knit to end of rnd.

RNDS 21–30: Work 6 sts of Right Chart B 2 times, work 6 sts of Right Chart A once, knit to end of rnd.

RNDS 31–40: Work 6 sts of Right Chart C once, work 6 sts of Right Chart B 2 times, work 6 sts of Right Chart A once, knit to end of rnd.

RNDS 41–49: P3, k3, work 6 sts of Right Chart C once, work 6 sts of Right Chart B 2 times, work 6 sts of Right Chart A once, knit to end of rnd.

Size 7½" (19 cm) only

RND 50: P3, work wrapped st over 3 sts, work 6 sts of Right Chart C once, M1P, work 6 sts of Right Chart B 2 times, work 6 sts of Right Chart A once, knit to end of rnd—31 instep sts.

For rem of sock to cuff, work instep sts as foll: Work 12-st rep of Right Chart D once, p1, work 6 sts of Right Chart B 3 times. Skip to Shape Gussets.

Sizes 9 (10½)" (23 [26.5] cm) only

RND 50: P3, work wrapped st over 3 sts, work 6 sts of Right Chart C once, work 6 sts of Right Chart B 2 times, work 6 sts of Right Chart A once, knit to end of rnd.

RNDS 51–59: [P3, k3] 2 times, work 6 sts of Right Chart C once, work 6 sts of Right Chart B 2 times, work 6 sts of Right Chart A once, knit to end of rnd.

Cont for your size as foll:

Size 9" (23) cm only

RND 60: P3, k3, p3, work wrapped st over 3 sts, work 6 sts of Right Chart C once, M1P, work 6 sts of Right Chart B 2 times, work 6 sts of Right Chart A once, knit to end of rnd—37 instep sts.

For rem of sock to cuff, work instep sts as foll: Work Right Chart D over 18 sts (first 6 sts of chart and 12-st rep), p1, work 6 sts of Right Chart B 3 times. Skip to Shape Gussets.

Size 10½" (26.5 cm) only

RND 60: P3, k3, p3, work wrapped st over 3 sts, work 6 sts of Right Chart C once, work 6 sts of Right Chart B 2 times, work 6 sts of Right Chart A once, knit to end of rnd.

RNDS 61–69: [P3, k3] 3 times, work 6 sts of Right Chart C once, work 6 sts of Right Chart B 2 times, work 6 sts of Right Chart A once, knit to end of rnd.

RND 70: P3, work wrapped st over 3 sts, p3, k3, p3, work wrapped st over 3 sts, work 6 sts of Right Chart C once, M1P, work 6 sts of Right Chart B 2 times, work 6 sts of Right Chart A once, knit to end of rnd—43 instep sts.

For rem of sock to cuff, work instep sts as foll: Work 12-st rep of Right Chart D 2 times, p1, work 6 sts of Right Chart B 3 times, knit to end of rnd.

SHAPE GUSSETS

At the same time, when sock measures 3½" (9 cm) less than desired length to back of heel, shape gusset as foll:

INC RND: Work instep sts as directed, sl m, k1, M1, knit to last st, M1, k1—2 sts inc'd.

Work 1 rnd even. Rep last 2 rnds 14 more times—60 (66, 72) sole sts.

TURN HEEL

Work heel turn back and forth using short-rows (see Glossary) as foll:

SHORT-ROW 1: (RS) Work instep sts to marker, k44 (50, 56), wrap next st, turn.

SHORT-ROW 2: (WS) P28 (34, 40), wrap next st, turn.

SHORT-ROW 3: Knit to 1 st before wrapped st, wrap next st, turn.

SHORT-ROW 4: Purl to 1 st before wrapped st, wrap next st, turn.

Rep Rows 3 and 4 nine more times—11 sts wrapped on each side; 8 (14, 20) sts rem unwrapped in center of heel.

HEEL FLAP

SHORT-ROW 1: (RS) Sl 1 pwise wyb, k17 (23, 29), working 10 wraps tog with wrapped sts, knit next wrap tog with wrapped st and next st on left needle (3 loops total), turn—1 gusset st dec'd.

SHORT-ROW 2: (WS) Sl 1 pwise wyf, p28 (34, 40), working 10 wraps tog with wrapped sts, ssp next wrap tog with wrapped st and next st on left needle (3 loops total), turn—1 gusset st dec'd.

SHORT-ROW 3: [Sl 1 pwise wyf, k1] 14 (17, 20) times, sl 1 wyb, k2tog, turn—1 gusset st dec'd.

SHORT-ROW 4: Sl 1 pwise wyf, p28 (31, 34), ssp, turn—1 gusset st dec'd.

Rep Rows 3 and 4 until 1 gusset st rem each side, ending with a WS row—63 (75, 87) sts: 32 (38, 44) heel sts, 31 (37, 43) instep sts.

Resume working in rnds as foll:

NEXT RND: [Sl 1 pwise wyb, k1] 15 (18, 21) times, work gusset st tog with first instep st (removing m and keeping to instep patt as established), cont as established to last instep st, work last instep st tog with next gusset st (removing m and keeping to instep patt as established), M1. Pm for new beg of rnd—62 (74, 86) sts rem.

NEXT RND: Work first 6 sts of Right Chart D, then 12-st rep 3 (4, 5) times, pm, p1, work 6 sts of Right Chart B 3 times, k1.

NEXT RND: Work Right Chart D as established to marker, p1, work 6 sts of Right Chart B 3 times, k1.

Cont in patt as established until sock measures about 2" (5 cm) less than desired finished length, ending with Row 10 of Right Chart B.

CUFF

RND 1: Work Right Chart D as established to m, p1, work 6 sts of Right Chart C 3 times, k1.

RND 2: Work Right Chart D as established to m, k2tog, k1, p4, work 6 sts of Right Chart C 2 times, k1—61 (73, 85) sts rem.

RNDS 3–8: Work Right Chart D as established to m, work 6 sts of Right Chart C 3 times, k1.

RND 9: Work Right Chart D as established to m, work 6 sts of Right Chart C 2 times, p3, k2, ssk—60 (72, 84) sts.

RND 10: Work Right Chart D as established to m, work 6 sts of Right Chart C 3 times.

NEXT RND: *P3, k3; rep from * around.

Rep last rnd until ribbing measures 1" (2.5 cm). BO in patt.

Finishing

Weave in loose ends. Block as desired.

escadaria socks

save your **socks**

by **Eunny Jang**

When you spend so much time knitting socks, the last thing you want is to lose them to a hole. Here's how to preserve them.

I believe in using handmade things, making them part of my everyday life, enjoying them as beautiful functional objects. Sadly, my Handmade Manifesto doesn't confer inviolability—if used, things wear out. That's where mending comes in.

The basic goals of any mending method are to contain the damage, preventing it from spreading, and to strengthen the weakened area (or create completely new fabric where there is none left).

There are two major methods for mending socks: Darning and Reknitting.

MATERIALS

✖ a **darning egg** or **mushroom** to slightly stretch the fabric under repair. An incandescent lightbulb or any other smooth-surfaced round item small enough to fit inside the sock will do in a pinch.

✖ a blunt **tapestry needle**.

✖ a few yards of **leftover sock yarn**. If you are very organized, you will have leftover yarn from each sock project wrapped neatly around a card kept in your sock drawer. If you are human, use any yarn with the same gauge and fiber content, matching the color (or not!) to your sock.

✖ To reknit, you'll also need smooth, **heavy-duty sewing thread** and a **hand-sewing needle**.

The classic darning method involves simple weaving.

Darning

This is your basic sock darn. The result is a patch that looks and feels quite noticeably different from the surrounding fabric, but is fast to work and reasonably strong.

1 Contain the hole. With a running stitch, outline a square area around the hole **(Figure 1)**. Note: To show the repair over the hole as clearly as possible, the rows between the box and hole have been omitted from the illustrations.

2 Make sure your repair box leaves at least three or four whole stitches or rows between it and the hole. You'll work your repair over all these stitches, making sure that the new fabric is firmly anchored in the old.

3 Weave across rows. Beginning at the lower right corner of the box, weave in and out of each whole stitch across a row of knitting. When you reach the left side of the box, bring the needle out half a row above the previous strand and return to the right side in the same way. Leave long strands across the hole, making sure not to draw the yarn too tightly **(Figure 2)**.

4 Weave up and down. Beginning at an upper corner of the box, weave in and out down a column of knitting. When you reach the bottom, bring the needle over half a stitch and return to the top in the same way **(Figure 3)**. When you reach the hole, work a simple weave—over one strand, under one strand—across the strands

stretched across it. Make sure the next pass of yarn moves through the strands in the opposite way— that is, under a strand that it went over on the last pass, and vice versa.

5 Weave in your tails.

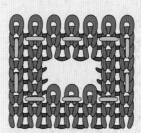

FIGURE 1

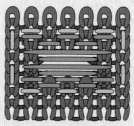

FIGURE 2

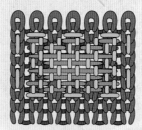

FIGURE 3

save your socks

Shown here in two colors, reknitting is generally imperceptible when complete.

Reknitting

Reknitting a hole is significantly more complicated than darning it, but it results in a beautiful, almost invisible repair that stretches exactly like the surrounding fabric. You'll be using a duplicate stitch to recreate the underlying fabric.

1 Using sewing thread, create a frame over the hole (**Figure 1**).

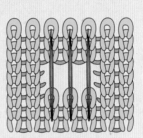

FIGURE 1

2 Beginning at the lower right corner at least three stitches and rows away from the lowest part of the hole, bring your sewing thread out in the center of a stitch. Making sure that it is traveling along a single column of stitches, catch one loop in the upper right corner and bring the thread straight back to where it started, bringing it down in the center of the stitch again. Bring it back up in the next stitch to the left, and across the hole (**Figure 2**).

Each pair of thread strands will anchor one column of stitches.

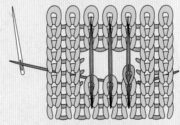

FIGURE 2

3 Begin working duplicate stitch (see next page) in the lower right corner of your thread frame (**Figure 3**).

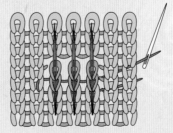

FIGURE 3

4 When beginning each stitch, come up between each pair of thread strands. Go over and underneath both to create the loop; go down between them again to end each stitch. While you have whole adjacent stitches, pass under and through them as you normally would for duplicate stitch.

5 Continue working duplicate stitch in continuous rows from right to left and back, working slowly from the bottom toward the top (Figure 3).

6 When you reach the hole, there will be no anchoring stitch above to pass through. Instead, just go underneath a pair of thread strands, making sure the loop has a reasonable gauge compared to the surrounding knitting. Continue splitting the pairs of threads at the beginning and end of each stitch.

7 When you reach the top of the hole, begin working into whole stitches as soon as possible. Continue working for at least two or three rows to anchor your reknitted area in stable fabric.

8 Clip and pull your thread strands; weave in yarn ends. Admire your newly mended sock!

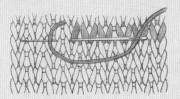

duplicate stitch

Bring the threaded needle out from back to front at the base of the V of the knitted stitch you want to cover. Working right to left, *pass needle in and out under the stitch in the row above it and back into the base of the same stitch. Bring needle back out at the base of the V in the next stitch to be covered. Repeat from * for the desired number of stitches.

 TIPS

* Prevent holes before they happen: consider carrying a reinforcing thread with the sock yarn as you knit high-stress areas such as heels and toes.

* Mend holey socks sooner rather than later; the smaller the hole, the faster, easier, and stronger the repair. You can even duplicate stitch over areas that are getting thin but haven't turned into a hole yet, to strengthen them.

* Both darning and reknitting will work best on flat, unshaped areas in your socks. If you need to fix a torn toe, pick up stitches in a complete round around the entire toe, rip out the old stitches, and reknit it completely. To reknit a heel, pick up stitches on the leg side and foot side.

* A quick-and-dirty fix for small holes in 100-percent wool socks: Lay a thin film of wool roving over the hole, extending a little bit onto the edges of the fabric. Needle-felt until secure, adding more roving as necessary. This felt patch will not be very elastic, so don't work it over an area that needs to stretch or cling.

glossary

ABBREVIATIONS

beg	begin/beginning	fptr	front post treble crochet	st(s)	stitch(es)
bet	between	fsc	foundation single crochet	tch	turning chain
blp	through back loop(s) only	g	gram(s)	tog	together
bpdc	back post double crochet	hdc	half double crochet	tr	treble crochet
bptr	back post treble crochet	hdc-cl	half double crochet cluster	tr-cl	treble crochet cluster
CC	contrasting color	incr	increase/increases/increasing	ttr	triple treble crochet
ch	chain	lp(s)	loop(s)	WS	wrong side
ch-sp	chain space	MC	main color	yd	yard(s)
cm	centimeter(s)	m	marker	yo	yarn over
dc	double crochet	opp	opposite	*	repeat instructions following asterisk as directed
dc-cl	double crochet cluster	pm	place marker	**	repeat all instructions between asterisks as directed
dec	decrease/decreases/decreasing	prev	previous	()	perform stitches in same indicated sts
dtr	double treble crochet	rem	remain/remaining	()	alternate instructions and/or measurements
ea	each	rep	repeat(s)	[]	work bracketed instruction specified number of times
esc	extended single crochet	rnd	round		
est	established	RS	right side		
fdc	foundation double crochet	sc	single crochet		
flp	through front loop(s) only	sh	shell		
foll	follow/follows/following	sk	skip		
fpdc	front post double crochet	sl st	slip stitch		

Bind-Offs

See also Bind-offs for Toe-up Socks, pages 112–115, for the following methods:

DOUBLED BIND-OFF

INVISIBLE SEWN BIND-OFF

KITCHENER BIND-OFF

SIDEWAYS BIND-OFF

JENY'S SURPRISINGLY STRETCHY BIND-OFF

This technique was originally published in *Knitty* and was developed by Jeny Staiman. It is a standard BO with a yarnover added before each st.

Keep work loose.

STEP 1: If the stitch to be bound off is a knit stitch, work a backward yo (bring yarn to the front over the needle **(Figure 1)**. Knit the next stitch, then insert left needle into yo and lift it over the knit stitch **(Figure 2)**.

If the stitch to be bound off is a purl stitch, work a standard yo **(Figure 3)**. Purl the next stitch, then insert left needle into yo and lift it over the purl stitch **(Figure 4)**.

STEP 2: Rep Step 1 for the second stitch to be bound off. Insert left needle in second stitch from tip of right needle and lift it over the next stitch.

Rep Step 2 until all stitches have been bound off. As you get into the rhythm of this method, you may prefer to lift the yo and the previous stitch over the next stitch together in a single motion **(Figure 5)**.

PICOT BIND-OFF

Using the standard method, bind off the first two stitches. *Turn work, use the knitted method (see page 161) to cast on three more stitches **(Figure 1)**, turn work, pass the second, third, and fourth stitches individually over the first **(Figure 2)**, so that one stitch remains on right needle **(Figure 3)**, then use the standard method to bind off the next two stitches. Repeat from *.

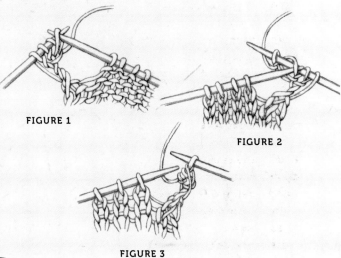

FIGURE 1

FIGURE 2

FIGURE 3

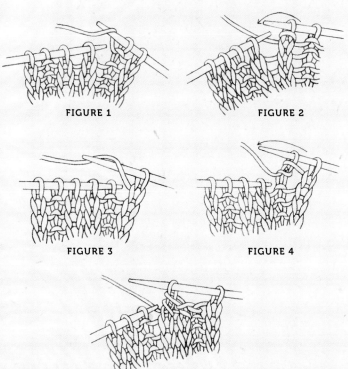

FIGURE 1

FIGURE 2

FIGURE 3

FIGURE 4

FIGURE 5

glossary

Cast-Ons

See also Cast-ons for Comfy Cuffs, pages 50–53, for the following methods:

OLD NORWEGIAN CAST-ON

CHANNEL ISLAND CAST-ON

ALTERNATING CAST-ON (also known as **ONE-ROW TUBULAR** or **ITALIAN**)

DOUBLE-START CAST-ON

See also Get Your Cast-On!, pages 36–41, for the following methods:

TURKISH/EASTERN CAST-ON

FIGURE-EIGHT CAST-ON

SQUARE TOE CAST-ON

CIRCULAR CAST-ON

SHORT-ROW TOE

CABLE CAST-ON

Begin with a slipknot and one knitted cast-on stitch if there are no established stitches. Insert right needle between first two stitches on left needle **(Figure 1)**. Wrap yarn as if to knit. Draw yarn through to complete stitch **(Figure 2)** and slip this new stitch to left needle to create a twist in the stitch as shown **(Figure 3)**.

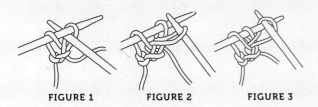

FIGURE 1   FIGURE 2   FIGURE 3

JUDY'S MAGIC CAST-ON

This amazingly simple cast-on is named for its founder, Judy Becker. It wraps the yarn around two parallel needles in such a way as to mimic a row of stockinette stitch between the two needles.

Leaving a 10" (25.5 cm) tail, drape the yarn over one needle, then hold a second needle parallel to and below the first and on top of the tail **(Figure 1)**.

Bring the tail to the back and the ball yarn to the front, then place the thumb and index finger of your left hand between the two strands so that the tail is over your index finger and the ball yarn is over your thumb **(Figure 2)**. This forms the first stitch on the top needle.

*Continue to hold the two needles parallel and loop the finger yarn over the lower needle by bringing the lower needle over the top of the finger yarn **(Figure 3)**, then bringing the finger yarn up from below the lower needle, over the top of this needle, then to the back between the two needles.

Point the needles downward, bring the bottom needle past the thumb yarn, then bring the thumb yarn to the front between the two needles and over the top needle **(Figure 4)**.

Repeat from * until you have the desired number of stitches on each needle **(Figure 5)**.

Remove both yarn ends from your left hand, rotate the needles like the hands of a clock so that the bottom needle is now on top and both strands of yarn are at the needle tip **(Figure 6)**.

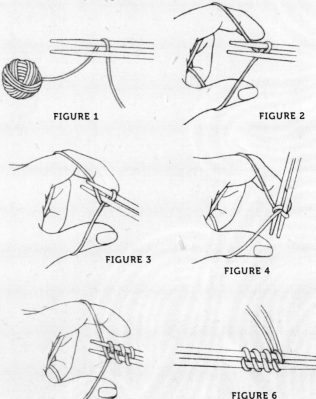

FIGURE 1   FIGURE 2

FIGURE 3   FIGURE 4

FIGURE 5   FIGURE 6

KNITTED CAST-ON

Make a slipknot and place it on the left needle (counts as first stitch). *With right needle, knit into the last stitch on the left needle **(Figure 1)**. Slip the stitch knitwise to the left needle **(Figure 2)**. Repeat from * for desired number of stitches.

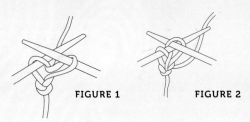

FIGURE 1   FIGURE 2

INVISIBLE PROVISIONAL CAST-ON

Place a loose slipknot on needle held in your right hand. Hold waste yarn next to slipknot and around your left thumb; hold working yarn over your left index finger. *Bring needle forward under waste yarn, over working yarn, grab a loop of working yarn **(Figure 1)**, then bring needle to the front, over both yarns, and grab a second loop **(Figure 2)**. Repeat from *. When you're ready to work in the opposite direction, pick out the waste yarn to expose live stitches.

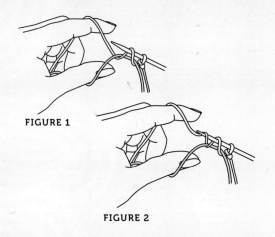

FIGURE 1

FIGURE 2

Decreases

SSP DECREASE

Holding yarn in front, slip two stitches knitwise one at a time onto right needle **(Figure 1)**. Slip them back onto left needle and purl the two stitches together through their back loops **(Figure 2)**.

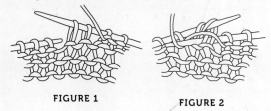

FIGURE 1   FIGURE 2

SL 2, K1, P2SSO

Slip two stitches knitwise **(Figure 1)**, knit the next stitch **(Figure 2)**, then use the point of left needle to pass the 2 slipped stitches over the knit stitch and off the right needle **(Figure 3)**.

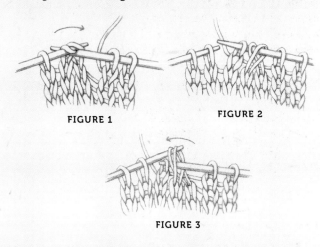

FIGURE 1   FIGURE 2

FIGURE 3

SL 1, K2TOG, PSSO

Slip 1 stitch knitwise, knit the next 2 stitches together, then use the point of left needle to pass the slipped stitch over the knit stitch and off the right needle.

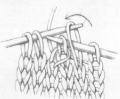

Grafting

KITCHENER STITCH

STEP 1: Bring threaded needle through front stitch as if to purl and leave stitch on needle **(Figure 1)**.

STEP 2: Bring threaded needle through back stitch as if to knit and leave stitch on needle **(Figure 2)**.

STEP 3: Bring threaded needle through first front stitch as if to knit and slip this stitch off needle. Bring threaded needle through next front stitch as if to purl and leave stitch on needle **(Figure 3)**.

STEP 4: Bring threaded needle through first back stitch as if to purl and slip this stitch off needle. Bring needle through next back stitch as if to knit and leave stitch on needle **(Figure 4)**.

Repeat Steps 3 and 4 until no stitches remain on needles.

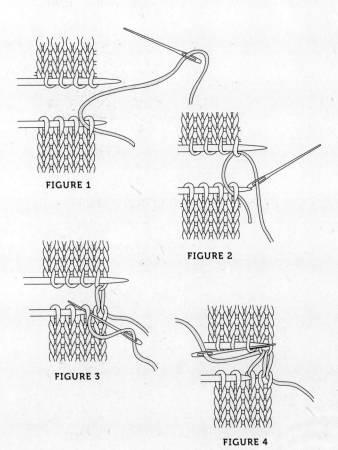

FIGURE 1

FIGURE 2

FIGURE 3

FIGURE 4

Increases

YARNOVER (YO)

Between Two Knit Stitches

Bring the yarn to the front between the needle tips, over the top of the needle, and to the back, ready to knit the next stitch.

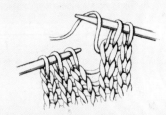

After a Knit, Before a Purl

Bring the yarn to the front between needle tips, over the top of the needle, and between the needles again to the front, ready to purl the next stitch.

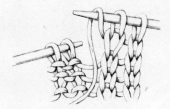

After a Purl, Before a Knit

Bring the yarn over the right-hand needle to the back, ready to knit the next stitch.

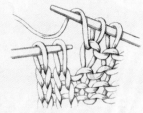

Between Two Purl Stitches

Bring the yarn over the right-hand needle to the back, then to the front again between the tips of the needles, ready to purl the next stitch.

RIGHT LIFTED INCREASE (RLI)

Knit into the back of stitch (in the "purl bump") in the row directly below the stitch on the left needle—one st inc'd.

LEFT LIFTED INCREASE (LLI)

Insert left needle from front to back into the stitch below stitch just knitted (**Figure 1**). Knit this stitch (**Figure 2**)—one st inc'd.

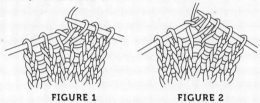

FIGURE 1   FIGURE 2

RIGHT LIFTED PURL INCREASE (RLPI)

Purl into the back of stitch in the row directly below the stitch on the left needle.

LEFT LIFTED PURL INCREASE (LLPI)

Purl into the stitch below the stitch just purled.

KNIT 1 FRONT & BACK (K1F&B)

Knit into the front (**Figure 1**), then the back (**Figure 2**) of the next st (one st inc'd). This produces an increase that resembles a knit st followed by a purl bump (**Figure 3**).

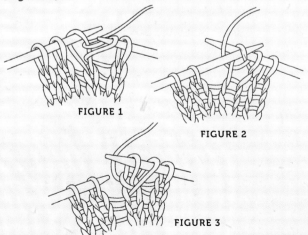

FIGURE 1   FIGURE 2

FIGURE 3

Make-One Increase

MAKE-ONE LEFT (M1L)

Note: When no direction is specified, use M1L.

With left needle tip, lift strand between needles from front to back (**Figure 1**). Knit lifted loop through the back (**Figure 2**).

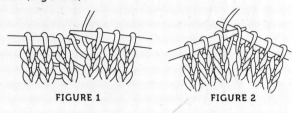

FIGURE 1   FIGURE 2

MAKE-ONE RIGHT (M1R)

With left needle tip, lift strand between needles from back to front (**Figure 1**). Knit lifted loop through the front (**Figure 2**).

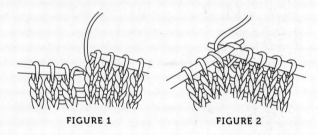

FIGURE 1   FIGURE 2

MAKE-ONE LEFT PURLWISE (M1LP)

Note: When no direction is specified, use M1LP.

With left needle tip, lift strand between needles from front to back (**Figure 1**). Purl lifted loop through the back (**Figure 2**).

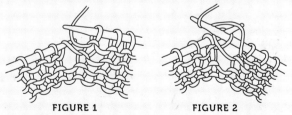

FIGURE 1   FIGURE 2

MAKE-ONE RIGHT PURLWISE (M1RP)

With left needle tip, lift strand between needles from back to front. Knit lifted loop through the front.

glossary

Pick Up and Knit

With right side facing and working from right to left, insert tip of needle under the front half **(Figure 1)** or both halves **(Figure 2)** of stitch along selvedge edge, wrap yarn around needle, and pull it through to form a stitch on the needle. For a tighter join, pick up the stitches and knit them through the back loop **(Figure 3)**.

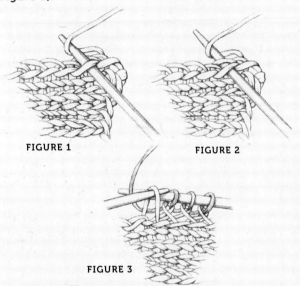

FIGURE 1

FIGURE 2

FIGURE 3

Short-Rows

KNIT SIDE: Work to turning point, slip next stitch purlwise with yarn in back, **(Figure 1)**, bring the yarn to the front, then slip the same stitch back to the left needle **(Figure 2)**, turn the work so the purl side is facing and bring the yarn in position for the next stitch—one stitch has been wrapped.

When you come to a wrapped stitch on a subsequent row, hide the wrap by knitting it together with the wrapped stitch **(Figure 3)**.

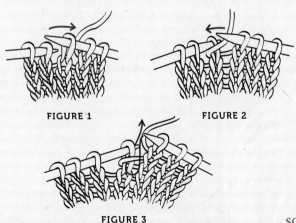

FIGURE 1

FIGURE 2

FIGURE 3

PURL SIDE: Work to the turning point, slip the next stitch purlwise with yarn in front, then bring the yarn to the back of the work **(Figure 1)**, return the slipped stitch to the left needle, bring the yarn to the front between the needles **(Figure 2)**, and turn the work so that the knit side is facing—one stitch has been wrapped.

To hide the wrap on a subsequent purl row, work to the wrapped stitch, use the tip of the right needle to pick up the wrap from the back, place it on the left needle **(Figure 3)**, then purl it together with the wrapped stitch.

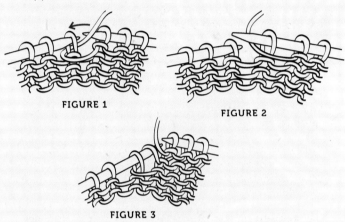

FIGURE 1

FIGURE 2

FIGURE 3

VARIATION ON HIDING A WRAP: When you come to a wrapped purl stitch on a subsequent knit row, hide the wrap by slipping the stitch and wrap together kwise to the right needle **(Figure 4)**. Insert the left needle into stitch and knit them together through back loops.

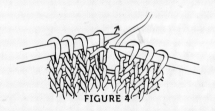

FIGURE 4

designers

COOKIE A is an avid sock knitter, teacher, and designer. Her patterns have been featured in *Vogue Knitting* and *Knit.1* magazines and *Knitty* online magazine. She teaches intensive sock design workshops internationally and is the author of *Sock Innovation* (Interweave). Visit her website at CookieA.com.

JUDY ALEXANDER lives in Longmont, Colorado, with her husband and two cats. She combines her love of knitting with her passion for fiber and color in her business TheKnitter.com, which she runs with her husband. In addition to knitting, Judy also enjoys spinning, weaving, and quilting.

STAR ATHENA lives in Portland, Oregon, where she is constantly inspired to knit and develop new designs. She likes to listen to records, daydream, and explore the Pacific Northwest.

KATE ATHERLEY is the technical editor of socks for *Knitty* and author of the books *Beyond Knit & Purl* and *Knit Accessories: Essentials and Variations*. Find her at her blog, Wise Hilda Knits.

DEB BARNHILL is a passionate knitter, designer, and teacher from Nova Scotia. Her designs have appeared in *Knitty* magazine, *Alpacas* magazine, and the books *Knitting Socks with Handpainted Yarns* and *Beyond Toes: Knitting Adventures with Judy's Magic Cast-on*. Find her online at www.knittingpharm.com.

When not entangled in yarn, **LORILEE BELTMAN** enjoys camping with her family and being on the water in small, non-motorized craft. She teaches continental knitting and other classes designed to make knitters try something new. Her family has recently moved from Michigan to Seattle.

STEFANIE BOLD's passion is knitting, but she also enjoys spinning, sewing, and other needle arts. She lives in Germany and blogs at hobbyatelier.blogspot.com.

CAT BORDHI is a teacher, author, knitter, designer, and forensic topologist. Visit her website, catbordhi.com, for books, patterns, and more, including her new ebook, *Cat's Sweet Tomato Heel Socks*.

ANN BUDD is a knitter, spinner, editor, and best-selling author. She lives in Boulder, Colorado, and blogs at annbuddknits.com.

Programmer by day, sock-knitting fanatic by night, **LESLIE COMSTOCK** longs for the day when she can devote herself to spinning, knitting, weaving, and dog walking.

Santa Cruz native **CLAIRE ELLEN** often knits at the beach. She has recently moved to Hungary, where she teaches English and enjoys learning about new yarn shops.

KAREN FRISA works as a freelance technical editor for Interweave and other companies. She teaches at Interweave Knitting Lab, Stitches events around the country, and at her LYS, K2TOG, near her new hometown of Berkeley, California.

CHRISSY GARDINER is a designer and teacher from Portland, Oregon, who has a special fondness for socks, lace, and textured colorwork. She is the author of *Toe-Up! Patterns and Worksheets to Whip Your Sock Knitting into Shape* and publishes the Gardiner Yarn Works line of patterns.

KRISTI GERACI started knitting while she was in grad school as a "cheap" hobby, and once she knit her first sock, she couldn't stop. In addition to designing, her other fiber pursuits include spinning, weaving, and sewing.

HUNTER HAMMERSEN recently abandoned the glamorous life of a grad student to write knitting books full time. Visit her blog, Violently Domestic, to keep up with her adventures.

TERRY MORRIS knits and designs patterns as she sails around the islands of the western Caribbean.

DEBORAH NEWTON lives in Providence, Rhode Island, where she has been designing knitwear as well as working in her family's business for many years. Her new book, *Finishing School*, professes her utter love for finishing and shares her "bag of tricks" for making the process painless.

SPILLYJANE (aka Jane Dupuis) lives in Windsor, Ontario, in a hundred-year old house with her husband and her avian companion, Pookie. She habitually translates her favorite things into elegantly quirky mittens and socks.

LISA STICHWEH designs, knits, and teaches in Mason, Ohio. She leads a bimonthly sock club there and can be found on her blog, *Stitch Ways*.

yarn sources

Abstract Fiber
3676 SE Martins St.
Portland, OR 97202
abstractfiber.com

Blue Moon Fiber Arts
56587 Mollenhour Rd.
Scappoose, OR 97056
bluemoonfiberarts.com

Cascade Yarns
PO Box 58168
1224 Andover Park E.
Tukwila, WA 98188
cascadeyarns.com

Dream in Color
dreamincoloryarn.com

Frog Tree Yarns
PO Box 1119
East Dennis, MA 02641
frogtreeyarns.com

Muench Yarns/GGH
1323 Scott St.
Petaluma, CA 94954
muenchyarns.com

Lion Brand
135 Kero Rd.
Carlstadt, NJ 07072
lionbrand.com

Lorna's Laces
4229 N. Honore St.
Chicago, IL 60613
lornalaces.net

Louet North America
3425 Hands Rd.
Prescott, ON
Canada K0E 1T0
louet.com

Malabrigo
malabrigoyarn.com

Plucky Knitter
thepluckyknitter.com

Plymouth Yarn
500 Lafayette St.
Bristol, PA 19007
plymouthyarn.com

Quince & Co.
quinceandco.com

Spinrite Yarns
320 Livingstone Ave. S., Box 40
Listowel, ON
Canada N4W 3H3
spinriteyarns.com

Spud & Chloë
Distributed by Blue Sky Alpacas
PO Box 88
Cedar, MN 55011
spudandchloe.com

The Verdant Gryphon
7923 B Industrial Park Rd.
Eston, MD 21601
verdantgryphon.com

index

Ann's Go-To Socks 8–11
Azurea Socks 12–17

bind-off methods
    Doubled (Decrease) 112
    Invisible Sewn 113
    Jeny's Surprisingly Stretchy 159
    Kitchener 114
    Picot 159
    Sideways 115

cable patterns 46–49, 54–61, 80–83, 96–99
Caret + Chevron Socks 18–23
cast-on methods
    Alternating (Tubular) 52
    Cable 160
    Channel Island 51
    Circular 39
    Double-start 53
    Figure-eight 37
    Invisible Provisional 161
    Judy's Magic 160
    Knitted 161
    Old Norwegian 50
    Short-row Toe 40–41
    Square Toe 38
    Turkish/Eastern 36–37
Cataphyll Socks 70–79

darning 155
decreases 161

Emerging Cable Socks 54–61
Escadaria Socks 146–153
eye-of-partridge patterns 132–141

flap heel 85–86
Flutterby Socks 28–35
Frost Feather Stockings 116–121

garter stitch Jacquard 100–107
grafting. See Kitchener stitch
grid patterns 146–153

increases 162–163
instep measurement 87

Kitchener stitch 162

lace patterns 116–121

magic loop technique 48, 56
Muscadine Socks 108–111

Oak + Acorn Socks 42–45
Our Paths Cross Socks 132–141

Passerine Socks 142–145
pick up and knit 164

reknitting 156–157
reversible patterns 18–23, 80–83, 84–86, 88–89
rib patterns 8–11, 24–27, 46–49, 96–99, 122–127, 146–153

Schwäbische Socks 122–127
self-striping yarn 24–27
short-row heel 85–86
short-rows 164
Simply Elegant Cable Socks 96–99
slip-stitch patterns 28–35, 108–111
sock toes 128–131
Sockupied history 7
Spectrum Socks 62–65
Speed Bump Socks 24–27
stranded color work 42–45, 62–65, 66–69
Sweet Tomato Heel 30, 32–33
symmetrical patterns. See reversible patterns

Thanks-Ma round 33, 34
Turnalar Socks 100–107
Twisted Diamonds Socks 46–49
twisted-stitch patterns 46–49, 122–127, 142–145

Uloborus Socks 90–95

vertical stranding 137

Wyeast Socks 80–83

Create one-of-a-kind socks
WITH THE HELP OF THESE INTERWEAVE RESOURCES!

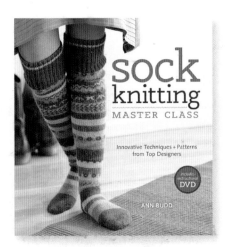

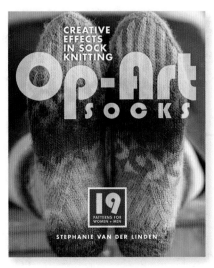

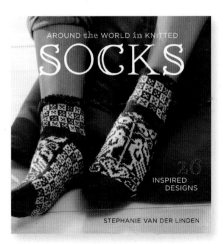

**SOCK KNITTING
MASTER CLASS**
Innovative Techniques +
Patterns from Top Designers

Ann Budd

ISBN 978-1-59668-312-9
$26.95

OP-ART SOCKS
Creative Effects in
Sock Knitting

Stephanie van der Linden

ISBN 978-1-59668-903-9
$24.95

**AROUND THE WORLD
IN KNITTED SOCKS**
26 Inspired Designs

Stephanie van der Linden

ISBN 978-1-59668-230-6
$24.95

Available at your favorite retailer or  knitting daily **shop**   shop.knittingdaily.com

---

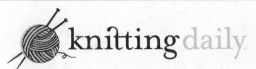

Join Knittingdaily.com, an online community that shares your passion for knitting. You'll get a free e-newsletter, free patterns, a projects store, a daily blog, event updates, galleries, knitting tips and techniques, and more. Sign up at Knittingdaily.com.

INTERWEAVE
KNITS

From cover to cover, *Interweave Knits* magazine presents great projects for the beginner to the advanced knitter. Every issue is packed full of smart, captivating designs, step-by-step instructions, easy-to-understand illustrations, plus well-written, lively articles sure to inspire. Interweaveknits.com